D0997954

01818536

African Arguments

African Arguments is a series of short books about Africa today. Aimed at the growing number of students and general readers who want to know more about the continent, these books highlight many of the longer-term strategic as well as immediate political issues confronting the African continent. They get to the heart of why Africa is the way it is and how it is changing. The books are scholarly but engaged, substantive as well as topical.

Series editors
ALEX DE WAAL, Social Science Research Council
RICHARD DOWDEN, Executive Director, Royal African Society

Editorial board
EMMANUEL AKYEAMPONG, Harvard University
TIM ALLEN, London School of Economics and Political Science
AKWE AMOSU, Open Society Institute
BREYTEN BREYTENBACH, Gorée Institute
CRAIG CALHOUN, Social Science Research Council
PETER DA COSTA, journalist and development specialist
WILLIAM GUMEDE, journalist and author
ALCINDA HONWANA, Open University
ABDUL MOHAMMED, InterAfrica Group
ROBERT MOLTENO, editor and publisher

Titles already published
Tim Allen, *Trial Justice: The International Criminal Court and the Lord's Resistance Army*

Alex de Waal, *AIDS and Power: Why There is No Political Crisis – Yet*

Raymond W. Copson, *The United States in Africa: Bush Policy and Beyond*

Chris Alden, *China in Africa*

Tom Porteous, *Britain in Africa*

Julie Flint and Alex de Waal, *Darfur: A New History of a Long War* (expanded and updated edition)

Forthcoming
Jonathan Glennie, *Aid and Africa: Getting it Right*

Peter Uvin, *Life after Violence: A People's Story of Burundi*

Published by Zed Books and the IAI with the support of the following organizations:

InterAfrica Group The InterAfrica Group is the regional centre for dialogue on issues of development, democracy, conflict resolution and humanitarianism in the Horn of Africa. It was founded in 1988 and is based in Addis Ababa, with programmes supporting democracy in Ethiopia and partnership with the African Union and IGAD. <www.sas. upenn.edu/African_Studies/ Hornet/menu_Intr_Afr.html>

International African Institute The International African Institute's principal aim is to promote scholarly understanding of Africa, notably its changing societies, cultures and languages. Founded in 1926 and based in London, it supports a range of seminars and publications including the journal *Africa*. <www.internationalafricaninstitute.org>

Justice Africa Justice Africa initiates and supports African civil society activities in support of peace, justice and democracy in Africa. Founded in 1999, it has a range of activities relating to peace in the Horn of Africa, HIV/AIDS and democracy, and the African Union. <www.justiceafrica.org>

Royal African Society Now more than a hundred years old, the Royal African Society today is Britain's leading organization promoting Africa's cause. Through its journal, *African Affairs*, and by organizing meetings, discussions and other activities, the society strengthens links between Africa and Britain and encourages understanding of Africa and its relations with the rest of the world. <www.royalafricansociety.org>

Social Science Research Council The Social Science Research Council brings much-needed expert knowledge to public issues. Founded in 1923 and based in New York, it brings together researchers, practitioners and policymakers in every continent. <www.ssrc.org>

TOM PORTEOUS

Britain in Africa

Zed Books
LONDON | NEW YORK

University of KwaZulu-Natal Press
PIETERMARITZBURG, SOUTH AFRICA

in association with

International African Institute
Royal African Society
Social Science Research Council

Britain in Africa was first published in association with the International African Institute, Royal African Society and Social Science Research Council in 2008 by:

in South Africa, University of KwaZulu-Natal Press, Private Bag X01, Scottsville 3209, South Africa, books@ukzn.ac.za

in the rest of the world, Zed Books Ltd, 7 Cynthia Street, London N1 9JF, UK and Room 400, 175 Fifth Avenue, New York, NY 10010, USA

www.zedbooks.co.uk
www.ukznpress.co.za
www.internationalafricaninstitute.org
www.royalafricansociety.org
www.ssrc.org

Cover designed by Andrew Corbett
Set in OurType Arnhem and Futura Bold by Ewan Smith, London
index: <ed.emery@thefreeuniversity.net>
Printed and bound in the EU by Gutenberg Press Ltd, Malta

Distributed in the USA exclusively by Palgrave Macmillan, a division of St Martin's Press, LLC, 175 Fifth Avenue, New York, NY 10010.

A catalogue record for this book is available from the British Library
US CIP data are available from the Library of Congress

ISBN 978 1 84277 975 0 hb (Zed Books)
ISBN 978 1 84277 976 7 pb (Zed Books)
ISBN 978 1 86914 149 3 pb (University of KwaZulu-Natal Press)

Contents

Acknowledgements

This book is not the product of academic research but of my experience as a journalist, diplomat and human rights activist working on Africa over twenty years. The book emerged from an article I wrote on British policy in Africa, published in *International Affairs* in March 2005. Richard Dowden, the Director of the Royal African Society, suggested that I turn the article into a book. I am indebted to him not only for his encouragement but also for his concise and insightful comments on the first drafts of the manuscript. I am also grateful to my other editors, Alex de Waal, Robert Molteno and Ellen McKinlay, for the time and effort they put into reading the manuscript and for their sharp and useful suggestions. Andrew Mawson, my colleague at Human Rights Watch, and Sally Healy, my former colleague at the FCO, were among several others who also very kindly gave up their time to read the manuscript and comment on it. Although I have greedily adopted many of the ideas and suggestions of my editors and other readers, I accept full responsibility for the analysis presented here as well as for any errors of judgement or fact. Finally I acknowledge a debt of gratitude to my parents, to my sons, and to my wife, Niloofar.

Abbreviations

AU	African Union
BAE	British Aerospace
BBC	British Broadcasting Corporation
CIA	Central Intelligence Agency
CPA	Comprehensive Peace Agreement (in Sudan)
DfID	Department for International Development
DR Congo	Democratic Republic of Congo
EC	European Commission
EU	European Union
FCO	Foreign and Commonwealth Office
G8	Group of Eight industrialized countries
ICC	International Criminal Court
ICU	Islamic Courts Union
IMF	International Monetary Fund
MoD	Ministry of Defence
NATO	North Atlantic Treaty Organization
NEPAD	New Partnership for African Development
NGO	non-governmental organization
OAU	Organization of African Unity
ODA	Overseas Development Administration
OECD	Organisation for Economic Co-operation and Development
RUF	Revolutionary United Front (Sierra Leone's rebel movement)
SPLA	Sudan People's Liberation Army
UN	United Nations

Introduction

At the time the Labour Party came to power in 1997, the incoming prime minister, Tony Blair, had hitherto indicated little interest in Africa and even less knowledge of African politics. But by the end of Blair's premiership ten years later, Africa had become a major theme and an explicit priority of Britain's foreign policy. The prime minister had sent British troops to Sierra Leone. He had more than tripled the UK's aid budget for Africa. He had forged close personal relations with several African leaders. He had convened and chaired a high-level Commission for Africa to propose solutions to Africa's developmental problems. And Blair had justified the UK's new prioritization of Africa not only on moral grounds, but also, after 11 September 2001, on strategic grounds: the spread of poverty, conflict and corruption in Africa, he argued, was not only creating misery for many Africans, it was also profoundly antithetical to UK interests because it was a fertile ground in which international crime and terrorism could flourish.

The first purpose of this book is to examine how and why this happened. What factors or combination of factors and events brought Africa to the forefront of British foreign policy during Blair's ten years in office? What were the influences, both within the government and outside it, which brought about this transformation? What events in Africa and in the world helped to shape the British government's policies towards Africa? What were the rationales for these policies? What was the interpretation of interests that lay behind them? And how did this interpretation of interests determine Britain's aims and objectives in Africa in this period?

The second purpose of the book is to identify what Britain's policies and strategies in Africa between 1997 and 2007 actually were and how they evolved. How did the UK government seek to achieve its aims and secure its objectives in Africa in areas of economic development and poverty reduction, counterterrorism and conflict prevention, democracy and human rights, energy security, trade and business? What international partnerships did it seek in pursuit of its aims? How did Africa policy fit into and inform wider efforts of the UK government to strengthen the international system, for example through UN reform, EU expansion and the creation of the International Criminal Court?

My third purpose is to assess the effectiveness of British policies in Africa in meeting their aims. How successful has the UK been in achieving its objectives and securing its interests? What have been the reasons for Britain's successes and failures in Africa? To what extent were decisions made on the basis of sound analysis of the problems the UK sought to address and of the influence and leverage that the UK could bring to bear to achieve its goals? How did the institutional apparatus of UK foreign-policy-making and the attitudes of those involved hinder or facilitate the implementation of British policies in Africa? And how has the UK managed to reconcile competing interests and objectives when they turned out (as they tended to) to be contradictory?

I should declare at the outset my own interest in British policy in Africa under Tony Blair. I served for three years in Whitehall as the conflict management adviser for sub-Saharan Africa in the Foreign and Commonwealth Office (FCO). I was recruited in 2000 to fill an FCO post that was created as part of the government's Africa Conflict Prevention Pool, a cross-departmental initiative designed to join up the UK's conflict management efforts in Africa and make them more strategic. The Pool (which had about £100 million to spend on conflict management activities in Africa per year) was managed by the Cabinet Office and involved the FCO, the Ministry of Defence (MoD) and the Department for International Development (DfID). My job was to represent and protect the FCO's departmental interests in this joint initiative – to ensure that the FCO's views were properly represented in the government's decision-making process with respect to the UK's conflict management activities in Africa. My qualifications for this work included almost a decade as a journalist writing and broadcasting (mostly for the BBC World Service) on African politics, particularly on armed conflicts in Africa, as well as a couple of assignments with UN peacekeeping operations in two of Africa's most intractable and violent conflicts: in Somalia in 1994 and Liberia in 1995.

Part of my motivation for joining the FCO was that I was impressed by the Labour government's attention to Africa in its first term. I was in particular encouraged by its commitment to conflict resolution and state-building, which was most remarkably demonstrated by the politically difficult decision to send British troops to help to stabilize Sierra Leone in 2000 after the UN peacekeeping effort there was threatened by a rebel coup. I stayed in the FCO for almost three years. But in March 2003 I handed in my resignation, in dismay and frustration over the UK's unqualified backing for what I saw as the United States government's counterproductive approach to counterterrorism, an approach that included the waging of an ill-considered war of choice in Iraq. In my resignation letter on 23 March 2007 I said that I believed that the invasion of Iraq was a serious strategic error that would increase instability in the region and in the world. I also predicted that it would seriously damage the UK's international reputation.

In spite of my ultimate disillusion with the broad direction of British foreign policy post-2001, I still believe that under sometimes very difficult circumstances, the UK has done some good

3

in sub-Saharan Africa under the Labour government. Furthermore my tenure in the FCO gave me a privileged view of British diplomacy in action: the obstacles, real and imagined, that stand in the way of doing some good in the world, and the various pressures placed on politicians by the media, pressure groups and lobbyists, the internal politics of Whitehall, the mediation of departmental interests and objectives, the filtering of information, analysis and intelligence – in short the complex process of decision-making in British foreign policy.

The structure of the book broadly follows the three sets of purposes noted above. Chapter 1 sketches out the institutional perspectives that led the key government departments and Number 10 Downing Street to make Africa a priority. Chapter 2 analyses the policy itself, including an analysis of the report of Tony Blair's Commission for Africa, and the broad strategies that made up the policy. Chapter 3 provides a critique of the policy as it was implemented. The fourth chapter provides a conclusion and makes some guesses as to the short-, long- and medium-term futures of the UK's relations with Africa.

1 | The players

'We have to concentrate on the things that really matter – what I call the big picture – not the periphery.' Tony Blair's first foreign policy speech at the Lord Mayor's Banquet, London, 10 November 1997

It is very unlikely that anyone could have foreseen in May 1997 that Tony Blair would pay more attention to Africa than had any British prime minister since Harold Macmillan. Macmillan, of course, was the prime minister who oversaw the dismantling of Britain's colonies in Africa. Blair by contrast led Britain back into Africa in a manner that was self-consciously interventionist and neo-imperialist, albeit justified in terms of partnership with African leaders and humanitarianism. But this was not part of any grandiose plan. New Labour came to power in 1997 with an only roughly formulated set of notions about what Britain's foreign policy should look like. Some liberal talk of a foreign policy with an 'ethical dimension' was balanced by reassuringly familiar statements about promoting British interests and values and maintaining a strong alliance with the United States. But the real test of any new government's foreign policy is in the making of it. To use Macmillan's phrase, it is 'events, dear boy, events', not predetermined plans, however well laid, which generally drive foreign policy. And it was events, in Africa and elsewhere, which prompted the Labour government to make decisions that gradually brought Africa to the forefront of its foreign policy.

When the new government came into office there were strong pressures on it not to rush into any new foreign policy initiatives, least of all in Africa. Both for the policy elite in the FCO and for the small group of advisers surrounding Blair, none of whom had much experience of African affairs, Africa was simply not on the radar. Britain's relationship with the continent was, with the exception of long-standing and important ties with South Africa, seen as economically and commercially insignificant. Britain had no obvious and immediate strategic and security interests south of the Sahara. And there were no politically burning issues (such as Rhodesia and South Africa's apartheid in the 1970s and 1980s) requiring urgent prime ministerial attention. From a British foreign policy perspective, therefore, Africa was marginal. The idea of a closer British engagement with Africa was never even entertained in the months following Labour's victory – and if it had been it would immediately have been discarded as a needless and senseless liability for a government whose main concern was to prove to the British electorate that it was in a safe pair of hands. The watchword on foreign policy was caution.

For most of the second half of the twentieth century Britain's relationship with Africa had been characterized by disengagement, withdrawal and damage limitation. In 1945 Britain emerged from the Second World War exhausted and bankrupt. The new Labour government of Prime Minister Clement Attlee believed that Britain's African colonies could help to regenerate Britain's economic fortunes. But Whitehall had not done the sums. Economic regeneration required investment in the colonies which the UK could not afford. As Britain lurched from one financial crisis to another in the post-war years, the political pressure for independence within the colonies grew, as did the administrative and military costs of maintaining them. There was also pressure from the United States, which was by now concerned that anti-colonial sentiment would open the door to the spread of Soviet influence in Africa. By the mid-1950s it was becoming clear to the government in London that it would have to accelerate its hitherto leisurely plans for political independence. The Suez crisis of 1956 removed any doubt about the feasibility of maintaining an African empire in the face of the 'winds of change'. In the next ten years Britain, like France, hastily headed for the exit in all its major African colonies.

The transition to independence in Britain's former colonies was everywhere traumatic and difficult, especially for the Africans. In several, including Sudan, Nigeria, Uganda and Rhodesia, it led quickly to political crises and bloody civil wars. In Malawi, Zambia, Kenya, Sierra Leone, Somalia (part of which was a former British colony) and Tanzania, hopes for representative government were dashed by the swift emergence of military dictators or one-party rule. Throughout the continent the UK sought to protect its strategic and commercial interests by maintaining protector–client relations with governments in its former colonies, usually with some success. In this effort the UK faced its most complex and difficult challenges in southern Africa, where there was the largest concentration of European settlers. Rhodesia declared unilateral independence in 1965, and came under the control of a white minority government. South Africa had ceased to be a British colony in 1910, but in 1948 the Nationalist Party came to power in whites-only elections and started to implement its repressive apartheid policies of racial discrimination. Thirteen years later South Africa relinquished its British dominion status and withdrew from the Commonwealth. Meanwhile the Portuguese colonial governments in Mozambique and Angola continued to cling on to power throughout the 1960s and early 1970s in the face of growing African insurgencies. Britain, in the retreat from empire, had little room for manoeuvre to manage these multiple crises. White settler lobbies, linked to British commercial interests, exercised considerable influence in Whitehall, in parliament and in the British press. Throughout southern Africa, the UK maintained extensive business interests which it was determined to protect. The cold war also intruded on British calculations as the Soviet Union and China sought to extend their influence in the region by supporting African nationalist movements. Juggling strategic, commercial and political interests in the face of these countervailing challenges in southern Africa was the overwhelming priority for the African diplomacy of successive UK governments, Conservative and Labour, from the 1960s until the end of the cold war.

By 1997, the contours of post-cold-war Africa were beginning to emerge, and they were far from promising. Much of the continent was in turmoil. In central Africa, the ramifications of the Rwandan genocide three years earlier were still being felt, especially in the Democratic Republic of Congo (formerly Zaire), where it had helped to spark a series of wars and tribal conflicts in which many of the states of the region were militarily involved and in which hundreds of thousands of people were to lose their lives over the next few years. Beyond the Great Lakes, the Horn of Africa was also a region of endemic conflict throughout the 1990s (as it had been in the cold war period). Somalia remained without a central government after its collapse in 1991. Since withdrawing UN peacekeepers in 1995, the UN Security Council had effectively washed its hands of the country, leaving the field wide open to others, including warlords and militant Islamist groups, to fill the power vacuum. Relations between Ethiopia and Eritrea were declining and heading, as it turned out, towards a border war in which tens of thousands of soldiers were slaughtered in two years of trench warfare. Sudan's long-running civil war between the Khartoum government and the southern rebels of the Sudan People's Liberation Army was worsening under the Islamist regime of Omar al-Bashir, sucking in regional and international players.

In West Africa, too, the mutually reinforcing conflicts that had been festering in Sierra Leone and Liberia since the start of the decade were undermining the security of the whole region. The month Labour came to power Sierra Leone suffered yet another *coup d'état* which overthrew the recently elected government. Côte d'Ivoire, Liberia's southern neighbour, had been a bastion of stability in West Africa. It too soon fell victim to the now familiar combination of regional destabilization, ethnic division and internal power politics. Nigeria, meanwhile, Africa's most populous state and an important oil producer, where the UK had significant commercial interests, had reached a nadir of corruption, political violence and internal repression under the military regime of General Sani Abacha.

In southern Africa, at least, there was some good news: the transition in 1994 from apartheid to democracy in South Africa had passed off peacefully, with significant input from British diplomacy. President Nelson Mandela, courted and fêted internationally, held out hope of political, economic and cultural renaissance both in his own country and in Africa more generally. Another southern African country, Mozambique, provided an example of how, given the right tools and political circumstances, the UN could help to nudge belligerents towards resolution of civil war. And Botswana showed that economic prosperity and political freedom could take root and flourish in African soil. Nevertheless, even in this region there were acute problems. Zimbabwe had won independence in 1980 under a UK-brokered deal between the minority white Rhodesian government and the rebels. Now it was beginning its descent into economic decline and political repression thanks to President Robert Mugabe's determination to cling on to power at all costs. And the long civil war between the government and rebels in Angola continued, its impact felt in neighbouring DR Congo and Namibia.

Africa's conflicts were having a devastating humanitarian impact. As in other conflict-prone parts of the world, the majority of the victims were civilians. Millions of Africans were displaced both within and across international borders. Massacres, sexual

9

violence, ethnic cleansing, abductions, starvation, forced labour, the recruitment of child soldiers: these tactics were used systematically by belligerents in conflicts throughout the continent as a means of securing strategic objectives. Besides violent conflict, Africa was beset by other serious problems: widespread poverty, corruption, high rates of illiteracy, environmental degradation (some related to global warming) and high mortality due to ill health, including epidemics of malaria, HIV and other fatal diseases.

The state of Africa in 1997 posed challenging moral, political and strategic questions to policy-makers in the West. What were the consequences for the rest of the world if political and economic conditions in Africa continued to deteriorate? What were the remedies for the perennial problems of corruption and poverty? How could African states be strengthened to prevent them from falling farther into political instability and conflict? What could external actors such as the United States, the Europeans and other concerned members of the United Nations do to help resolve existing conflicts and to improve Africa's economic and political prospects? What were the diagnoses of the problems and the political and financial costs of effective solutions? How far were internal factors to blame for Africa's problems, such as the corruption of African elites or 'ingrained' paternalist and patrimonial political structures? How far were external factors responsible, such as the cold war and colonial legacies, the uneven terms of economic exchange between Africa and the West, debt, the exploitation of Africa's resources, or global warming?

The Conservative government had not seriously engaged with these issues in the first half of the 1990s. Apart from their role in South Africa, neither the Foreign Secretary, Douglas Hurd, nor Prime Minister John Major had given much attention to Africa or seriously sought to reframe British policy there in the light of the end of the cold war. Lynda Chalker, the long-serving

Conservative minister responsible for overseas development, had developed close relations with a number of African leaders and was interested in African politics. But she carried little weight within the government. The Conservatives were happy to claim some of the credit for the transition from apartheid to democracy in South Africa. But they studiously avoided getting any more deeply involved in the emerging African crises of the 1990s than the UK's permanent membership of the UN Security Council demanded. As long as it was able to protect Britain's business interests, especially in South Africa, the UK government was content to leave it to the multilateral organizations, the UN agencies, the international financial institutions and the European Commission to work out the broader international development, humanitarian and conflict management policies.

When the new Labour government took over in mid-1997 there was no immediate move to reverse this hands-off approach to Africa. Two early decisions by the Labour team, however, helped to set the stage for the increased British engagement that would occur over the next decade. One was the decision taken before the election, and included in the party's election manifesto, that if Labour won power it would create a department for international development independent of the FCO. It was hard to see how a government department devoted to humanitarianism, economic development and poverty reduction could avoid making Africa its main focus of attention. The other was the decision of the new Foreign Secretary, Robin Cook, to announce that the Labour government would pursue a foreign policy with a distinctively 'ethical dimension'. Here too was an initiative which, if implemented, was bound to lead Britain to engage with a continent whose widespread poverty, conflict and misery, many argued, demanded an ethical and humanitarian response.

Both these decisions – the creation of DfID and the announcement of a more 'ethical' foreign policy – were influenced by a number of disparate factors. First there were the distinctly old Labour internationalist currents which still flowed quite deeply in the party and with which Robin Cook and Clare Short, who was appointed as the new Secretary for International Development, were both loosely aligned. Although Blair and his close advisers were wary of these trends, it was none the less politically expedient to accommodate them to avoid alienating the left of the party. The Blairites probably calculated that it was easier and less risky to accommodate such tendencies in overseas development policy, and even in some non-security-related areas of foreign policy, than in the politically more sensitive areas of domestic social and economic policy. It is significant that Blair appears to have hesitated at the last minute about implementing the election manifesto pledge to create DfID, and was only persuaded to stick to the plan under strong pressure from Clare Short.[1]

Another factor that determined the decision to create DfID, and may have influenced Cook's ethical foreign policy initiative, was the growing clout of overseas development and humanitarian NGOs like Oxfam and Christian Aid. These organizations were traditionally pro-Labour. Some of them had worked in the run-up to the election to acquaint the future Labour leadership with their concerns. Oxfam had even taken Cook on a trip to Rwanda in 1996, just two years after the genocide, an experience that Cook later said had moved him greatly.[2] Furthermore these NGOs had been at the forefront of Western efforts to address the mounting humanitarian crises of the early 1990s, many of which were in Africa. This had increased their media profile and their ability to speak with authority on Africa's problems. The NGOs also had distinct ideas about how to tackle the longer-term economic problems of Africa, for example through increased development assistance, debt relief and the removal of trade barriers. They were keen to use their influence with the new Labour government and more widely to get these ideas put into action, and wasted no time in putting pressure on Parliament, Downing Street, DfID and the FCO to that end. The most high-profile instance of this NGO activity was the formation of the Jubilee 2000 campaign for debt relief in November 1997, which also demonstrated to the new government the power of NGOs to mobilize grassroots support and mass action.

A third influence in these early days of the Labour government came from public opinion and the media. Even though Africa hardly dominated the news agenda in the 1990s, the media could not ignore the great upheavals and transformations that were taking place in the continent in places such as Rwanda, Somalia, Ethiopia, Sudan and South Africa. Humanitarian crises in Africa were starting to impinge on public opinion in Britain in very direct ways thanks to the immediacy of satellite communications and twenty-four-hour news broadcasting. At a time of growing economic prosperity in the UK, a media image of Africa was emerging of a continent beset by poverty, conflict and crises. Journalists who reported on these disasters depicted a continent uniquely in need of international assistance and even of military intervention.

In retrospect, it did not require much analysis, observation and imagination to realize that it was wrong to regard Africa as marginal to Britain's longer-term interests. Whether the state of Africa improved or deteriorated, it was already clear that the continent was becoming more central to international security and therefore to the interests of the UK and Europe than ever before. Increasing numbers of African refugees and economic migrants, many of them escaping very real dangers and hardship in their home countries, were washing up, dead or alive, on the north coasts of the Mediterranean. The influx of clandestine and legal immigrants and asylum seekers was changing Europe's ethnic, social and political make-up and thus providing fodder for increasingly popular right-wing political parties with overtly racist agendas. In the 1990s the immigration issue became one of the central political themes in most European states, especially in Britain.

By the 1990s the USA and the Europeans both had good reason to be concerned also about the way in which international criminal cartels involved in drugs smuggling, people trafficking, arms dealing and other criminal activities were becoming well established in the conflict zones of Africa. West Africa was taking over from the Caribbean as the main transit point for the flow of drugs from South America to European markets. Furthermore, to those who followed Islamist movements before 11 September 2001, it was already clear in the decade before the al-Qaeda attacks in New York and Washington, DC, that anti-Western Islamist militancy was finding a foothold on the continent. Sudan had been taken over by an Islamist regime in 1989 and the government there was not only seeking to export its ideology to the rest of the Muslim world, but was playing host to Osama Bin Laden and his followers. Somalia and Kenya were touched by Islamic radicalism, as were Africa's two most populous nations, Ethiopia and Nigeria. In the degraded conditions of several African states the potential was even there, according to some intelligence reports, for the continent to play a facilitating role in the transfer of nuclear material and technology to terrorist organizations.[3]

Of course, Africa held out positive potential for foreign interests as well. Cheap labour made it an attractive base for multinational companies, if only stability could be guaranteed. Africa had important reserves of minerals, some of which, for example coltan, had become essential ingredients in mass-production high-tech communications products like mobile telephones and computer games consoles. The continent was also an increasingly important source of oil and gas at a time when on the one hand industrialized and industrializing nations were competing more keenly among themselves for control of world energy reserves, and on the other hand the traditional sources of energy in the Middle East were seen as threatened by growing political instability. Furthermore, although many parts of Africa were indeed mired in armed conflict and poverty, this did not mean that economic activity was at a standstill or that African markets and economies were not growing. On the contrary, there were important economic opportunities for international business not only in areas of peace and relative prosperity, such as South Africa, but also in areas of conflict, poverty and instability, such as Nigeria, Angola, Sudan and Sierra Leone.

Back in 1997 such arguments, positive and negative, for greater British engagement in Africa still had to be developed. But the evidence on which they were based was already accumulating. Gradually, over the next few years and from its different institutional perspectives, Whitehall was to come around to the idea that Africa was indeed important and would develop policies to address what it came to see as crucial interests on the continent.

Development as foreign policy

DfID came into existence at a time of considerable soul-searching in Britain and elsewhere about the overseas development policies of the so-called 'donor governments' of the industrialized world. It was a debate that was influenced by a wide range of actors, including the major multilateral development organizations such as the World Bank, the International Monetary Fund, the Organisation for Economic Co-operation and Development (OECD), the European Commission (EC) and UN agencies, as well as the major development NGOs like Oxfam and Christian Aid, and the increasing number of academic institutes, think tanks and university departments that specialized in development studies. Inevitably there were different strands of

15

opinion and theory and different interpretations of the political and economic forces at work on the ground in Africa. There were also outright dissidents who believed, following the work of the economist Peter Bauer, that it was fundamentally wrong to believe that transfers of cash from economically developed countries to economically underdeveloped ones could generate economic development.[4] This had not occurred anywhere else, these sceptics argued, so why should it occur in Africa? The evidence of the previous decades in Africa itself seemed to suggest they had a point.

The consensus of opinion within the development community was that, if overseas development aid had generally not produced economic development in previous decades, this was because its main purpose was strategic rather than economic. In the context of the cold war economic aid, like military aid, was provided mainly in order to secure and cement political and strategic alliances. How Britain's or America's allies in Africa, dictators like Mobutu Sese Seko in Zaire or Daniel arap Moi in Kenya, actually used that aid was not something which the donors had in the past been too concerned about. As long as these African big men stayed loyal, Western diplomats and politicians would turn a blind eye if much of the aid was siphoned off into overseas bank accounts or spent on useless white-elephant projects. In some cases Western companies were themselves aiding and abetting the corruption and profiting from it. Donor governments could not of course admit it out loud, but it was generally felt that, freed from the strategic constraints of the cold war, there was now an opportunity to get serious about how they went about providing development assistance and to design development strategies that had a chance of doing what they set out to do: helping poor countries to improve their economic performance and to reduce poverty.

Without doubt the need was very great in much of Africa.

Economic statistics in Africa are notoriously unreliable. But an observant visitor to Africa in the mid-1990s, as now, did not need statistics to see that the overwhelming majority of people in most African countries were desperately poor. Nor was it hard to identify many of the sources of that poverty: corruption, armed conflict, failing bureaucracies and administrations, limited political and economic freedom and governments lacking legitimacy. The donors correctly perceived that what was therefore needed was wholesale economic and political reform, and from the mid-1980s they set about putting pressure on African governments to accept and implement such reforms. But the devil was in the detail. It is one thing for a government to hold multi-party elections and to adopt a programme of economic structural adjustment because it knows that it has to do this to appease the donors and qualify for further grants and loans. It is quite another thing for a government to work in the spirit of those reforms to ensure that they lead to a vibrant democratic society and a well-functioning economy. The experience of much of the 1990s was that in most cases economic and political reforms were implemented only on the surface. Indeed, in some cases the reform programmes designed by economists at the World Bank and elsewhere (designed, it should be said, with more respect for free market ideology than for the realities of African political economies) may even have served to increase poverty and inequality and to push states farther to the brink of crisis and conflict. The problem was that the most negative features of African states were not accidental. Powerful political elites deliberately nurtured corruption and dysfunctional administrations precisely because these apparent aberrations suited their interests. The political entrepreneurs who controlled African states benefited from the apparent chaos, and even from armed conflict. There was method in the madness of a Liberia or a Zaire. Such countries worked very well for those who ran them. Doling

17

out foreign aid to these elites while failing to acknowledge or address the reality of what was going on behind the façade of the state could actually make matters worse, not better.

The donors, of course, were unwilling to accept any blame themselves for the failure of the reform programmes of the late 1980s and early 1990s. But they could hardly ignore the fact that these programmes had failed. So they settled on governance as the main culprit. This was a polite way of saying that African governments were themselves at the heart of the problem. And this was certainly part of the story: it was impossible to implement political and economic reforms in the context of weak states with corrupt rulers who, even if they did hold multi-party elections from time to time, generally lacked political legitimacy. Besides governance, the development establishment, comprising both donor governments and development NGOs, identified a number of other issues that they believed they needed to tackle if they were to fine-tune their development interventions and make them more effective. One was trade: African products needed to be allowed to compete on a more level playing field in world markets. Another was investment: far more was needed in Africa to help stimulate and sustain economic growth. A third issue was debt: this was holding African economies back and needed to be reduced or, better still, cancelled. A fourth was conflict: economic development and poverty reduction could not take place unless current conflicts were resolved and future conflicts prevented. And a fifth issue was aid itself: the current levels of aid were totally inadequate to stimulate economic growth; much, much more needed to be provided; and it needed to be delivered in a more effective and coordinated way. But important as these issues were, little could be achieved unless the governance failures of African states were addressed.

Even without the creation of a separate department of state dealing with international development, the UK government would have had to engage with and respond to the intellectual and ideological debates on development taking place in the mid-1990s at the World Bank, the OECD, the EC and in the major NGOs. But now there was DfID. In Clare Short it had a pushy and outspoken secretary of state at its helm with a seat at the cabinet table. The new department was busy recruiting large numbers of new civil servants, many of them from the NGO world, who brought confidence and idealism to their new government jobs. DfID was also promised significant new funding from Gordon Brown, the new Chancellor over at the Treasury, who shared Short's faith in the effectiveness of aid. And, most importantly, DfID was freed from the tutelage of the FCO, whose diplomats not only looked down their Oxbridge noses at their red-brick-university-educated, sandal-wearing colleagues in development, but also (to the annoyance of Short) tended to regard development assistance as of little value except as a lever for securing political and commercial objectives.

Short soon started to make her presence felt both in Whitehall and in the international development community. As a first step she latched on to the OECD's recently developed international development targets – the so-called Millennium Development Goals – and commissioned a White Paper designed to focus UK development policy on the international effort to meet those goals.[5] Thus poverty reduction became the department's over-arching goal. Eventually this focus on poverty reduction was to be enshrined in the 2002 International Developmemt Act. Soon DfID was at the centre of a host of international debates and initiatives on how to achieve poverty reduction where it was needed most: in Africa. Predictably, DfID quickly adopted the recommendations of the emerging consensus of the development community: that what was needed was more and better-focused aid, debt relief, more investment, a fairer deal for African trade and a big push to tackle poor governance and conflict. The recommendations that

DfID adopted dovetailed neatly with the institutional interests of the new department, which was looking not only for more money to spend but also for justifications to extend its brief into new and exciting policy areas such as security and diplomacy.

One predictable outcome of the creation of DfID was that Africa quickly became its number one priority. Another was that it soon ran into conflict with other departments of state, notably the FCO and the MoD. The question quickly emerged: who controlled British policy in Africa? In the past, when DfID's predecessor, the Overseas Development Administration (ODA), was a part of the FCO, the FCO's predominance was clear. However much importance the ODA may have given to development in Africa, the department's subordination to the FCO (for which Africa was not a priority) meant that the FCO's concerns (and those of the MoD) would always trump those of ODA officials and ministers. With the creation of DfID, however, development assistance was explicitly untied from the promotion of British commercial and strategic interests, and the priorities of the UK's development policy in Africa got a hearing at cabinet meetings, a more strategic focus and a lot more cash. These dynamics soon ensured that most important aspects of Britain's policy in Africa were determined and dominated by DfID and Clare Short. Because Short cared more about Africa than any of her cabinet colleagues, because she had a strong moral argument that went down well with both old Labour and new, and because she could pull rank over the junior ministers and government officials who dealt with Africa at the FCO and the MoD, she generally got her way. If the FCO was particularly concerned about the way DfID was dealing with an African issue, for example concerns about the governance and human rights record of proposed recipients of UK aid, it had to rely on persuasion and complex Whitehall manoeuvres to make sure its concerns were acted on. Usually it was just not worth it. So gradually Britain's policy in Africa was taken over by a department whose main mission was not diplomacy but development policy.[6]

From an international and presentational perspective this was welcome. An ethical UK policy towards Africa with poverty reduction at its heart was a worthy goal. It set Britain apart from other former colonial powers in Africa such as France and Italy, as well as from the United States, which continued assiduously to pursue their own interests on the continent as they had in the past. From now on the UK's approach to Africa at international conferences and at the EU and the UN was to be aligned more with that of the Nordic European countries, which for some time had put the accent on social and economic development. But from an internal institutional perspective the ascendancy of DfID over the FCO created a serious problem. Just at the moment when the donors began to recognize the importance and central-ity of governance to successful economic development, the UK government was transferring decision-making on Africa from a department that had the political and diplomatic skills and tools to improve governance to one that did not.

An early example of where this could lead came after Short vis-ited Rwanda in 1998. She quickly came to the view that the West, including the UK, had failed Rwanda during the 1994 genocide in which some 800,000 people, mostly Tutsis, were massacred. She argued that the failure of the UN and others to prevent the genocide or to intervene to stop it was a negligence that verged on complicity and left a huge burden of responsibility on the West to help Rwanda to recover from the disaster. During her visit to Rwanda Short observed that the Rwandan government of Paul Kagame (with whom she was immensely impressed and struck up a strong rapport) was still struggling to rebuild the country. The parlous state of the economy meant that it was being denied international finance. She determined to step in with UK assistance.[7] Almost overnight the UK became Rwanda's largest bilateral provider of economic aid – and a protector of a government that was already deeply implicated in other regional conflicts, in particular in the DR Congo.

In locking the UK into a large programme of economic assistance to the new Tutsi-dominated government, Short was also locking the UK into taking Rwanda's side in the wider conflict in the Great Lakes region. Rwanda was already deeply implicated in a complex, fast-moving and deadly war in the DR Congo. Although Rwanda had good strategic reasons to intervene in this conflict its conduct was by no means without fault. It stood accused of hunting down and murdering tens of thousands of Hutu refugees, including women and children, who had fled Rwanda in 1994. Its troops were in control of much of eastern DR Congo and were not above stirring up violent ethnic conflicts in pursuit of Kigali's objectives. There were also persistent reports, endorsed by several UN investigations, of the involvement of Rwanda and Uganda (another recipient of considerable quantities of UK development aid) in the illegal and abusive exploitation of economic resources in DR Congo – exploitation that prolonged the conflict and the suffering of millions of Congolese. Furthermore, the Rwandan government's record at home was far from benign. It regularly locked up its political dissidents, including a former president, for long periods. It suppressed free expression and it manipulated elections to exclude opponents from the political arena. But the more aid DfID poured into Rwanda the less Clare Short was inclined to hear criticism of Kagame, let alone use the threat of cutting aid as a means of demanding a change in Rwandan policy. The accusations against Rwanda were serious enough that the situation was potentially very embarrassing for the British government, and doubly so because soon much of Britain's aid was in the form of direct budget assistance (direct transfers of money) and therefore fungible. It was quite possible to argue, as several critics did, that UK taxpayers' money was being used to support Rwanda's abuses both at home and in DR Congo.

The overriding consideration for DfID was that Kagame was performing well in helping the department to achieve its development targets. He was, according to DfID's research, doing a good job in reducing poverty, in increasing girls' access to education, improving the health infrastructure in rural areas, etc. This trumped all other considerations, including human rights and regional stability. As far as the former were concerned, Short appeared to believe that it was sometimes necessary to sacrifice human rights for the greater good, which in this case was defined by DfID. As for regional stability, she appeared genuinely to believe that Kagame, like Yoweri Museveni in Uganda, and Ethiopia's Meles Zenawi in the Horn of Africa, was a force for good in his region and that his presence in DR Congo was necessary, justified and stabilizing. This approach raised eyebrows in the FCO. But central Africa was hardly the top concern for Britain's top diplomats and no one was prepared to pick a fight with Short over the issue.

Institutional tensions between the FCO and DfID over Africa policy persisted in Whitehall because the question of who controlled the policy was never fully resolved, in spite of mechanisms established by the Cabinet Office, such as the Africa Conflict Prevention Pool, designed to coordinate policy and allow mediation of departmental interests. In her memoir Short says that the FCO 'took every possible opportunity to brief against us and to use their private secretary in Number 10 to overrule us'.[8] But it was not just about clashes of departmental cultures and personalities (though there were plenty of those). As more and more resources were poured into DfID to tackle the challenges of development in Africa, over at the FCO there were substantial cuts in staff and resources devoted to Africa. This dynamic fundamentally changed the whole British approach to Africa and the character of its presence on the ground. This was not all a bad thing. DfID's claims that the FCO was stuffy and anachronistic were sometimes on the mark. But there were substantial drawbacks too. DfID did not have a broad enough view of the continent. Its resources and staff were deployed only in those countries where it had a major aid programme, and it therefore had little institutional understanding of what was going on in the rest of Africa. The FCO did not have embassies in every African capital but at least it had a remit to cover political and economic developments in the whole continent and to scan the horizon for emerging opportunities and threats. As cuts were imposed on the FCO, embassies closed and political analysts were given early retirement. The capacity of the UK government to gather the information and do the analysis on which to base its policy declined.

It was not just foreign policy which suffered from the declining resources the FCO had available for Africa. Development policy suffered too. The challenges of development in Africa are essentially political in nature, and the failures of development policy in the past have usually been failures of political analysis. DfID may have had the financial and technical resources to manage its aid programmes in Africa, but it did not have the political and analytical resources, nor the linguistic skills, required to ensure that these programmes were put in their political and cultural context, and to prevent aid from being hijacked and manipulated by recipient governments and NGOs. Nor could DfID simply buy in the expertise – though it tried. It was not just a question of experts. It was a question of systems and structures, systems and structures that the FCO had spent years developing and which DfID just did not have.

An ethical approach to foreign policy?

Labour came to power at a time when the Foreign and Commonwealth Office was still seeking to redefine the UK's interests in the post-cold-war world. At the end of the 1980s and the start of the 1990s there was a mood of cautious optimism in Whitehall about the impact of the end of the cold war on global security. The collapse of Soviet power presented real opportunities. Western influence expanded rapidly into areas that were previously under the thumb of the Soviets. Democracies and free markets quickly emerged in eastern Europe and the Baltic states. And there were real hopes of peace dividends elsewhere – in the former Soviet republics of South Caucasus and Central Asia, in Russia itself, in the Middle East and in Africa.

In Africa the end of the cold war did have some positive effects. Much-delayed political and economic reforms were fast-tracked in several African countries. In 1990 both Douglas Hurd, the British Foreign Secretary, and François Mitterrand, the French president, declared their countries' support for democracy, the rule of law and human rights in Africa. This was a sharp reversal of policy for the two leading former colonial powers which had bankrolled more than a few repressive African regimes since independence. In response to external pressure, there were halting moves from dictatorship towards multi-party democracy in states such as Tanzania, Kenya, Zaire, Zambia, Malawi, Ghana, Cameroon, Benin, Côte d'Ivoire, Togo, Mali, Senegal and elsewhere, though some were more genuine and successful than others.

The end of the cold war also removed one of the main justifications for continuing white minority rule in South Africa and was one among many factors which convinced the apartheid government of F. W. de Klerk to open negotiations with the African National Congress (ANC). These led to South Africa's first elections under universal suffrage in 1994. In Mozambique the peace settlement between the previously Soviet-backed government and the South African-backed rebels was one of the early fruits of the changing geostrategic environment. In Angola the former pro-Soviet government, once backed up by Cuban forces, quickly made friends with South Africa and the West, which had hitherto supported Angola's rebel leader, Jonas Savimbi, in the civil war. Angola became a reliable if corrupt business partner for Western oil companies eager to take advantage of the country's massive oil reserves. Meanwhile retired South African soldiers who had once provided Savimbi's rebels with military back-up were taken on as mercenaries by the Angolan government to help defeat their erstwhile ally. In Ethiopia, the collapse of Soviet power hastened the removal of the Moscow-backed Derg regime by a combination of Eritrean and Tigrayan liberation movements which pragmatically toned down their own Marxist ideology in order to attract support from the West.

In spite of the positive global impacts of the end of the cold war, the security environment remained a cause of concern to the FCO in the 1990s. As the cold war confrontation between the United States and the Soviets receded, new security threats emerged. Initially these were correctly seen as far less serious than the threats that existed in the era of superpower confrontation. Nevertheless, a watching brief was required to deal with the threats of nuclear proliferation, terrorism, the growing influence of militant Islam (which was now exacerbating some long-running security problems, such as the Israel–Palestine conflict and the Kashmir conflict), the spread of epidemics, global warming and mass migration. There were also concerns about the fast-increasing economic power of China (though the issue of Chinese economic investment and trade in Africa was as yet not on the radar).

One of the most pressing concerns and challenges for the FCO in the early 1990s was the emergence of an increasing number of internal civil wars which in several parts of the world were exposing the inherent weakness of the states where they were taking place. This phenomenon was not entirely new, but it became more of a worry after the end of the cold war, which had hastened the disintegration or violent reconfiguration of a number of states. These small wars were challenging the whole basis of international security, predicated as it was on the functioning of the state system. Left unaddressed, or addressed in the wrong way, the internal dynamics of state disintegration could become quite acute and lead to the total collapse or fragmentation of states. The experience in the Balkans showed just how much international energy, effort and time were needed to deal with these threats if they were to be contained and eventually neutralized. But it also showed how internal conflicts could become regional ones, and how the weakening of state structures provided opportunities for non-state actors with agendas quite antithetical to the interests of the UK and other Western states.

In Africa the cold war had left a particularly unstable legacy. As noted, it was in Africa that some of the most terrifying examples of post-cold-war state collapse were to be found: Somalia, Liberia, Sudan, Angola, Ethiopia, Sierra Leone, Guinea, Zaire, Rwanda, Chad, to name but the worst. The roots of these conflicts lay in part in the policies of the cold war superpowers and their allies. For years the UK, France, the United States and the Soviet Union had promoted their strategic and commercial interests in Africa at the expense of African stability and human rights. If many African states were corrupt and weak it was partly because Western and Soviet policies had nurtured corruption and instability in pursuit of their interests in the post-colonial era. Long-running civil wars in Sudan, Mozambique, Angola and Ethiopia had been fomented and prolonged for years by the logic of superpower rivalry, with each side generously arming its proxies. On the rare occasions when interstate war broke out, as for example between Ethiopia and Somalia in the 1970s, it was inevitable that the superpowers should be involved. There were also frequent armed interventions by foreign troops, French, Cuban, American, Soviet, Belgian and British, to prop up their allies. Mercenary forces were

One

dispatched to carry out coups or foment unrest. Over the years there were mysterious assassinations of troublesome politicians in Kenya, Congo, Morocco and elsewhere, in which Western intelligence agencies were rumoured to have been involved. Blind eyes were discreetly turned to the egregious abuses of allies, such as Jonas Savimbi in Angola, Robert Mugabe in Zimbabwe, Daniel arap Moi in Kenya, Hissene Habré in Chad and others, to name but a few. Billions of dollars were looted from state coffers by national leaders in Zaire, Nigeria and elsewhere under the noses of Western diplomats. The practice had continued into the 1990s, when the extent of complicity of Western banks in providing safe haven for looted state resources from Africa was exposed amid general embarrassment.

These abuses, perpetrated, nurtured or tolerated by the West and its Soviet rivals, were never seriously acknowledged, let alone investigated. Rather they were ignored, denied or explained away in the name of cold war realpolitik. Thus it was not a sense of guilt or responsibility which drove the early efforts to address the worst manifestations of the cold war legacy in Africa but the notion of humanitarianism, and that proved to be rather a weak impulse. The first major crises of state collapse in Africa in the post-cold-war era were in Somalia and Liberia, and neither received the attention it deserved. The Liberian meltdown was initially left to a regional West African peacekeeping force led by the Nigerians to sort out. In Somalia the Americans intervened with a stabilization force in 1993. But the intervention was badly planned and badly executed. Within a year the United States was bogged down in a lethal conflict which ominously foreshadowed some of the problems US forces were to encounter ten years later in Iraq. Instead of staying the course, President Bill Clinton withdrew a year later, mission unaccomplished, handing over to an equally ill-prepared UN peacekeeping force, which itself was withdrawn in 1995.

After this failure it became clear that, whatever its role in generating African crises, the West was, for the time being at least, unlikely to expend the same amount of resources in stabilizing Africa as it was in addressing conflicts closer to home, for example in the Balkans. Africa was simply not seen as strategically important enough to warrant the expense in blood and treasure, as the UN secretary-general of the time, Boutros Boutros-Ghali, an African himself, pointed out at the time with bitterness. The ideals of humanitarianism were not enough to justify putting Western troops in harm's way, even to prevent the Rwandan genocide of 1994. For the rest of the 1990s, the United States and the UK preferred to secure their interests, sometimes in competition with the French and often at the expense of long-term stability, through local African proxies: the Nigerian-led regional peacekeeping forces in Liberia and Sierra Leone, local allies in the Great Lakes region (Kagame's Rwandan Patriotic Front and Museveni's Uganda), and later the African Union in Burundi, Darfur and Somalia. When it was necessary to resort to UN peacekeeping forces in Africa, it was generally Africans or South Asians who provided the boots on the ground.

Robin Cook arrived in the FCO in May 1997 with little experience or knowledge of Africa. At the time the FCO's geographical priorities lay elsewhere – in the Balkans, Iraq, the Middle East and Europe. Cook therefore tended to delegate the FCO's African business to officials and junior ministers and this, as already noted, helped to ensure that DfID soon dominated most day-to-day African business. Nevertheless, Cook was keen to make his and the UK's mark on a number of international cross-cutting issues that were of direct relevance to Africa. These included arms export control, landmines, small-arms proliferation, human rights, environmental protection, international peacekeeping and conflict prevention.[9] Cook saw to it that the FCO's work on human rights, democratization and 'good governance' was expanded. Experts and practitioners were brought into the FCO from NGOs such as Amnesty International and from the media to broaden the FCO's perspectives on these issues. An annual FCO human rights report was launched on the model of a similar report put out by the US State Department. Arms export controls were tightened. In an early example of UK cultivation of celebrity involvement in foreign policy initiatives, the FCO put its weight behind the NGO campaign for a ban on landmines, in which Princess Diana in the last year of her life was a major player. Under Cook's leadership the FCO also engaged more actively in building the capacity of the international system to address the emerging 'new wars' that were so well exemplified by the burgeoning conflicts in Africa.[10] Thus Britain became an active supporter of efforts to reform the UN to enable it to play a more effective role in peacekeeping, conflict prevention, post-conflict peace-building, human rights monitoring and protection of civilians in armed conflicts. The UK also became a champion of the NGO initiative to create an International Criminal Court to try perpetrators of the most serious crimes against humanity. Furthermore, Cook was one of the most pro-European of Blair's senior ministers, and he was determined that the UK should be in the forefront of European efforts to develop a common EU foreign and security policy. In a continent where EU effectiveness had long been hampered by the residue of colonial Franco-British competition and rivalry, this held out good potential.

Cook's new foreign policy was ambitious. It would require a great deal of diplomatic effort and international negotiation to realize it. But it had important and potentially beneficial implications for Africa. The agenda did indeed have the makings of a foreign policy with an ethical dimension. It was unfortunate, however, that Cook allowed his advisers explicitly to spin his policy as an 'ethical foreign policy' in the first weeks of his tenure. Presented in this way the initiative raised hackles in the FCO by suggesting that until now officials had been implementing an unethical foreign policy. More importantly, announcing an ethical foreign policy immediately set impossibly high standards for the new government's handling of foreign and diplomatic affairs.[11] It was only a matter of time before the FCO would be exposed as failing to meet those high ethical standards.

The first test came almost immediately when in May 1997 the British government banned Nigerian aircraft from flying into the UK on safety grounds. The move had been in the pipeline since long before the general election and the reasons were quite valid. Because of corruption in the Nigerian airline industry, Nigerian airlines did indeed have a terrible safety record and many of their planes were not airworthy. But Sani Abacha, the military ruler of Nigeria, interpreted the move as politically motivated and indicative of a new, perhaps ethical, UK policy towards his own regime. He therefore responded by banning British Airways from flying to Nigeria. The British dithered, and then quietly backed down, lifting the ban on Nigerian flights without any safety improvements being implemented.[12] The incident raised an important question: what would an ethical foreign policy towards a country like Nigeria look like?

Nigeria was a serious and serial abuser of human rights. Its military government was extremely repressive and showed little sign of being willing to give up power. The country was also mired deep in corruption, and this appeared to be facilitating the work of international criminal groups and money launderers. The hanging of the Ogoni environmental activist Ken Saro Wiwa in 1995 had provoked international outrage, not only against Nigeria (which was suspended from the Commonwealth) but also against the multinational oil companies which were seen as complicit in the abuses of the government in the Niger Delta. NGOs and the media were demanding that credible international pressure be put on Abacha to go. And there were practical as well as moral grounds for action: Abacha's misrule appeared to be driving the

31

country and the West African region towards economic and political catastrophe. Europe and the United States had important commercial interests in Nigeria (mainly oil), however, and were unwilling to use an oil embargo as a lever of change. Furthermore Nigeria itself had leverage over the West because it was leading and bankrolling regional peacekeeping forces in Liberia and Sierra Leone on which the West was pinning its hopes for regional security. In the event the new Labour government, for the time being at least, maintained much the same attitude towards Nigeria as that of the outgoing Conservative government. So much for an ethical foreign policy.

The new UK government's dilemma over Nigeria was soon solved, not by any skilful diplomacy on the part of the FCO, but by the death of Abacha in June 1998 and the start of a process of transition to democratic civilian rule. But the next African test of the new Labour government's ethical foreign policy was not so easily or quickly resolved. In 1998 it was revealed that FCO officials had the previous year given their approval to a shipment of arms to forces loyal to the president of Sierra Leone, Tejan Kabbah. At the time of the shipment Kabbah and his government were in exile in neighbouring Guinea, having being ousted in a coup in May 1997 by a coalition of Sierra Leonean rebels and dissident junior army officers. The arms shipment had been organized by a private British military company called Sandline International, whose chief executive, Tim Spicer, was a former British lieutenant colonel. The arms deal had been brokered by an Indian businessman called Rakesh Saxena. The transfer of weapons to Kabbah loyalists seeking to bring the ousted president back to power quite clearly breached a UN arms embargo that had been imposed on Sierra Leone. Following a tip-off, British customs officials launched an investigation, prompting Sandline's lawyers to send a fax to the FCO which stated among other things that the FCO had approved the arms deal. It was when this fax was leaked to the press that the whole murky affair came to light, seriously undermining the credibility of Cook's 'ethical foreign policy'. It did not help the FCO that both Spicer, who went on to win the main contract to provide private security services to the Americans in Baghdad, and Saxena, who has spent the past decade fighting extradition from Canada to Thailand on charges of embezzlement, were colourful figures who made the story all the more appealing to the media.

The 'arms to Africa affair', as it became known, was one of the first blunders of the new government's foreign policy. In retrospect it seems a somewhat quaint and typically British scandal. A public inquiry found that the problem was incompetence in the FCO rather than deliberate wrongdoing.[13] In any case, by the time the scandal came to light Kabbah had been restored to power, not with the help of Sandline's illegal arms shipment but by the UN-mandated West African peacekeeping force led by the Nigerians. The affair pales in comparison both to the scandals that have emerged in France over the corrupt dealings of French politicians in Africa and to the later distortions perpetrated by the UK and the United States over Iraq. It was significant, however, because it drew Tony Blair into the African arena for the first time, and may well have influenced Britain's pivotal decision to send troops to Sierra Leone a couple of years later, when the country's government was once again threatened by a rebel coup.

Another former British colony in Africa presented an even bigger political test for the new Labour government than either Sierra Leone or Nigeria, and one for which, it soon became clear, there would be no early or easy solution. Zimbabwe's crisis had its roots in an acute spiral of economic decline from the mid-1990s onwards (Zimbabwe became the world's fastest-shrinking economy), the increasing use of brutally repressive methods by the government to maintain its political ascendancy, an unresolved political problem of land ownership (70 per cent of Zimbabwe's best agricultural land was owned by about 4,500 white farmers), and the unpopular military involvement of the Harare government in the war in DR Congo. Because of Britain's position as the former colonial power and because of its historic commitments to assist financially with the politically charged process of land reform, the UK government could not avoid getting entangled in the crisis. Furthermore, thanks to the prominent role of the white farmers (most of whom were of British origin), Zimbabwe received more UK media and parliamentary coverage and comment than all the other African crises of the time combined. The performance of the new Labour government in handling the crisis there was thus under intense scrutiny. In the event the government managed to maintain a more or less principled position with regard to Zimbabwe. Its main objectives were the holding of free and fair elections, an end to the abusive tactics of the Mugabe government and a peaceful and equitable resolution of the land issue. Nevertheless, London remained wholly unable to influence events in Zimbabwe for the better. This was not only because Mugabe was able to exploit any criticism by British politicians to his own domestic advantage but also because the UK government was unable to persuade South Africa and other southern African governments to take a common stand against Mugabe's repressive behaviour. The crisis in Zimbabwe was an early demonstration for the new Labour government of its limited leverage in Africa and therefore of the risks of making Africa a foreign policy priority.

The big picture

Tony Blair arrived in 10 Downing Street with no practical foreign policy experience and little knowledge of Africa. He did, however, come with charisma, an almost missionary zeal to change the UK and the world for the better, and the kind of political clout that only a vast parliamentary majority can buy. Whether or not

Britain's senior civil servants, soldiers and spies welcomed this as a refreshing change from the weakness of the last years of John Major's Conservative government (and many clearly did), they all understood immediately and intuitively that Blair was going to be around for at least two terms and that they had better help him do what he wanted to do.

Blair's claim in a valedictory speech in South Africa in 2007 that Africa had been his priority since the beginning of his premiership was misleading. In fact, at the beginning Africa was nowhere on Number 10's agenda and Blair's advisers were keen that it should stay that way. It was not until 1999 that Blair first set foot in Africa as prime minister. Significantly he went to South Africa, to strengthen the UK's only commercially significant bilateral relationship on the continent and to tie up a defence contract. For the Labour spin doctors the visit was designed to cement Blair's public relationship with Nelson Mandela, who was stepping down as president but remained an international icon. The rest of Africa, which at this time was in the depth of its misfortunes, did not feature high on Number 10's agenda for the visit, nor did the issue of economic development. During the visit Alastair Campbell, Blair's influential press spokesman, was overheard quipping 'we don't do hot countries'. And Clare Short later reminisced in her memoir that she told her officials at about this time that 'they could be as radical as they liked' because over at Number 10 Campbell had no interest in DfID's efforts in the developing world.[14]

In the first months of the Labour government some subtle differences emerged on foreign policy between Cook and Blair. When Cook set out his priorities in his mission statement he talked up ethical issues like arms export control, human rights and the environment.[15] But he made no mention of the UK's relationship with the United States, an omission which was clearly deliberate and did not go unnoticed. Blair, on the other hand,

The players

35

from the start of his premiership, adopted a more conventional approach to foreign policy, at least rhetorically. In November 1997, in one of his first set-piece foreign policy speeches, delivered in white tie and tails at the Lord Mayor's Banquet, Blair said he intended to rely on the British armed forces and the alliance with Washington to promote 'the values and aims we believe in'.[16] In what was clearly a sideswipe at Cook's initiative on arms control, Blair also made it clear that he was averse to doing anything that would undermine British commercial interests, including the arms trade. Clearly for Blair promoting the British arms trade was one of the values and aims he believed in. In the course of his premiership he would go to great lengths to defend Britain's main arms exporter, BAE, even at the cost of accusations of covering up bribery and corruption and of undermining DfID's efforts to reduce poverty in Africa.

On foreign policy Blair was from the start a 'big picture' man. He didn't have time for the detailed analysis and often infuriated FCO officials by his failure to take note of their painstakingly drafted briefings or to heed their 'points to raise' in meetings with his international interlocutors. But Blair was interested in the bigger theories of international relations, such as those put forward by one of his early foreign policy advisers, Robert Cooper, a diplomat who argued that traditional concepts of international relations were being challenged by two opposing trends: the emergence of 'postmodern' states (the main example being the states of the European Union), which based their prosperity and stability on the concept of mutual cooperation and a dilution of sovereignty; and the emergence in parts of the underdeveloped, poor world of 'pre-modern' failing states whose sovereignty had collapsed from within.[17] According to Cooper, the 'postmodern' states of the EU, together with 'modern states' like the United States and Japan (which pursued old-fashioned 'balance of power' foreign policies), would have to resort to a kind of a benign imperialism in order to deal with the threats to global security – terrorism, weapons of mass destruction and failed or rogue states – which were emanating from the 'pre-modern' world. Needless to say Africa, according to this taxonomy, was pre-modern and thus ripe for the neo-imperialist approach. Blair's foreign policy soon fitted quite neatly into this theoretical modelling of international affairs. But, as the experiences of Iraq and to some extent Afghanistan were to show, it was hard to make the neo-imperialist approach work in practice, let alone reconcile it with human rights and liberal values.

Blair's reaction to the Sierra Leone 'arms to Africa' affair gave an early indication of his big-picture approach to foreign policy. Whereas Cook saw quite clearly that Britain had broken the law by approving the shipment of arms, which violated the terms of a UN arms embargo, Blair suggested that it was the UN arms embargo, which the British had drafted, which was at fault, and that Britain had done the right thing. While Cook was squirming with embarrassment at the scandal that was filling the front pages and blaming his officials for their incompetence, Blair went on the offensive with a bid for the moral high ground. 'Don't let us forget', he said at the time, 'that ... the UN and the UK were both trying to help a democratic regime [of president Kabbah] restore its position from an illegal military coup. They were quite right in trying to do it ... That is the background and people can see that a lot of the hoo-ha is overblown.'[18]

In the first two years of his premiership Blair authorized UK military action twice: first in 1998/99 in Iraq, where the UK joined the United States in Operation Desert Fox, a series of massive air strikes; and second in the 1999 Kosovo crisis, where the UK joined NATO in forcing Serbia, through a sustained military campaign, to withdraw its troops from Kosovo. During this period Blair was developing his thinking on international relations and in particular on the use of military force. He came to the conclusion that the rules of military intervention needed to be rewritten. On a visit to Chicago in April 1999 he went public with these ideas in a speech to the Chicago Economics Club in which he set forth what he called his 'doctrine of international community'. 'We are all internationalists now,' he said. 'We cannot turn our backs on conflicts and violations of human rights in other countries if we still want to be secure.'[19] He then proceeded to lay out the conditions in which he felt that military intervention was justified, necessary and a moral duty. The FCO, which had barely been consulted on the contents of the speech before it was delivered, was seriously alarmed about its ramifications.[20] Not only did the speech appear to question some of the basic tenets of international law, it also ignored the considerable work that was already being done on the issue of humanitarian intervention at an international level.[21] Nevertheless, the speech was widely praised across the political spectrum for its forthrightness and candour. Among those who applauded it was the band of neoconservatives in the United States which had already captured the Republican Party's foreign policy think tanks and was hoping to win the White House in the 2000 presidential election.[22]

Blair's Chicago speech made no mention of Africa, but an acute observer could hardly have heard it without suspecting that Blair's argument would sooner or later lead him into the continent, where so many of the conditions he laid out for military intervention seemed to be met. In 2000 Sierra Leone's hapless President Kabbah was in trouble yet again. Lacking sufficient resources to defeat the rebels, who were backed by Liberia's warlord-turned-president Charles Taylor, Kabbah was forced by the US government's special envoy and mediator Jesse Jackson into a power-sharing arrangement with the rebel Revolutionary United Front (RUF), which was to be guaranteed by the presence of a UN peacekeeping force. But quite predictably the Lome peace agreement failed. Taylor and the rebels wanted more. In April and May 2000, the RUF made their bid for power, attacking the UN and holding several hundred of them hostage. The crisis once more threatened the credibility of the UN at a time when it was being called on more than ever to help resolve African conflicts. Tony Blair ordered in British troops ostensibly at first to protect British and other foreign expatriates. But quickly the mission became as much political as humanitarian. The very presence of the British military, it soon became clear, was shoring up Kabbah's government and the UN operation. Then a maverick quasi-criminal gang called the West Side Boys, which had taken advantage of the chaos in Sierra Leone to carve out their own small zone of influence, kidnapped several British soldiers. British special forces dispatched to rescue them killed twenty-five of the kidnappers, including three women. After this impressive, not to say brutal, show of force, the RUF capitulated.

The military operation was a test of Blair's evolving philosophy of humanitarian intervention, and it was quickly depicted as a resounding success. The ramped-up military objectives were achieved with a minimum of casualties. Kabbah's government was rescued. The campaign (if that is not too grand a word) brought kudos to Britain and to Blair himself, not only among Sierra Leone's traumatized population but in Africa and internationally. The British press and public opinion, which had initially been sceptical about the dispatch of troops to a distant and tiny tropical country where Britain had no obvious interests beyond its status as the former colonial master, were duly impressed. For Blair it was a personal victory at home as well as a British victory abroad.

The Sierra Leone intervention focused Blair's mind for the first time on the problems of state collapse and failure in Africa, and brought him face to face with the challenge of post-conflict reconstruction and state-building. The relatively quick success of Britain's military operation convinced him that Africa was worthy of his attentions, a place where he could make a big difference without too much risk or cost. Those around him who insisted that New Labour did not 'do hot countries' were losing the argument. And there were other influences on Blair that were pushing him to make Africa more of a priority. The extraordinary charisma of Nelson Mandela, a champion of Africa's regeneration whom Blair met on several occasions and with whom at first he struck up a reasonably good rapport, certainly had an impact on him. Clare Short says that Blair was also influenced by the positive things he heard at international meetings about the work that DfID was doing in Africa. The claim is backed up by Blair himself, who went on record in Parliament to say that DfID's work was one of his government's proudest achievements.[23] There was also the pressure from humanitarian NGOs backed up, importantly, by the activism of rock stars such as Bono and Bob Geldof, whose success in raising awareness of poverty in Africa appealed to Blair's populist instincts and his belief in leveraging celebrity as a means of promoting a policy. Furthermore Bill Clinton, on his last visit to London as US president, told Blair that he regretted not having done more for Africa, and advised the prime minister to pay more attention to the continent in Labour's second term.[24] It is also clear that Blair's deep religious convictions as a professed and practising Christian moved him to address the urgent needs of a continent whose predicament so clearly called for a moral response. Blair's Christianity was famously downplayed by Alastair Campbell. 'We don't do God,' Campbell told a reporter who had tried to question Blair on his religious convictions during an interview.[25] But there is strong evidence that religion increasingly influenced Blair's foreign policy decision-making – including his tendency to see complex international issues in stark Manichaean terms.

Blair's biographers have noted that his religious convictions not only shaped the moral content of his foreign policy but also influenced an approach to decision-making on foreign issues which did not allow for much doubt or circumspection. Confronted with the big moral questions such as those posed by Iraq, the Middle East peace process and the sorry state of much of Africa, Blair's faith gave him the reassurance that he needed that the decisions and choices he made – many of them difficult – were the right ones. Once he had taken a decision, complexity and detail, even reality, could not get in the way of his determination to 'stay the course'. It was an approach that brooked little dissent on issues of high policy. In this sense, as one of his biographers has noted, Blair's faith 'narrowed him and made him less willing to listen'.[26] Blair knew best on Africa because he was right, just as he knew best on Iraq because he was right. It was an attitude that was neatly exemplified in a phrase in Blair's last speech on Africa in May 2007: 'Wealthy nations and Africa both face a choice: us, as to how far we help Africa to take the right path; Africa as to which path to take ... Our challenge is to support the good; Africa's challenge is to eliminate the bad.'[27]

Blair embarked on his second term in mid-2001 armed with an arsenal of moral arguments to make Africa a top priority for his government. Less convincing to the general public and to Blair's foreign policy advisers alike were the arguments that it was in Britain's strategic interests to shore up what the *Economist* magazine at about this time dubbed, on one of its covers, the 'Hopeless Continent'.[28] As already noted, there was evidence to suggest that Africa's ills could have a negative impact on Western interests. But the prevailing view in Whitehall and in the media was that Africa's problems could largely be contained in Africa. Not even the terrorist attacks on the US embassies in Nairobi and Dar es Salaam changed that perception. For one thing most of the victims were Africans and for another the attack was seen as a Middle Eastern-inspired operation with little relevance to Africa itself. But for Blair, as for many others, the al-Qaeda attacks on New York and Washington, DC, on 11 September 2001, fundamentally altered the perception of the radical Islamist threat. Henceforth no political leader in the West could afford to assume that the threat was anything other than urgent and global. It needed to be tackled on all continents, especially those with large Muslim populations living in fragile and failing states. Africa qualified well in those respects and quickly came into view as a strategic theatre for what the US administration was soon calling the 'global war on terror'. Within days of September 11, Washington was training its sights on a number of targets in Africa, including Somalia, a failed state, Sudan, an Islamist-run state that had hosted Osama Bin Laden in the 1990s, and the 'ungoverned spaces' of the Sahara, as possible targets for counterterrorism operations.

Blair was the first Western leader publicly to recognize the significance of Africa in the unbalanced and uncertain geostrategic environment that emerged in the aftermath of the al-Qaeda attacks. Speaking days after September 11 at the Labour Party conference, he said Africa was 'a scar on the conscience of the world' that would become 'deeper and angrier' unless something was done to heal it.[29] All of a sudden the prime minister who preferred the big picture to the detail had a compelling strategic argument of self-interest for dealing with Africa's many problems to add to his moral ones.

Business as usual?

As part of its bid for power in the run-up to the 1997 elections the Labour Party had worked assiduously to convince the captains of British industry and business that their interests would be well taken care of under a Labour government. Several prominent business leaders, out of conviction or opportunism, declared their confidence in Labour's business-friendly credentials well before the election. By 1997, less than ten years after the fall of the Berlin Wall put the nail in the coffin of socialism as a realistic alternative to capitalism, Labour had stolen the Conservative Party's clothes as the UK's party of business. It was never in doubt that although Labour did have a progressive social reform agenda both at home and abroad, this was to be implemented squarely within the context of a flourishing free market, capitalist economy. The new Chancellor of the Exchequer, Gordon Brown, quickly moved to show not only that New Labour was ideologically aligned with the leaders of Britain's largest enterprises, but that he personally was an 'Iron Chancellor', more than competent for the job of keeping the British economy on a sound footing.

Africa was not the main focus of British business concerns in the decade from 1997. As noted, much of the continent was marginal to British commercial interests. The exception was South Africa, far and away the largest market in Africa for British exports. In 2005 UK exports to South Africa totalled £3.2 billion, and UK investments in South Africa were estimated at £24 billion. The UK's economic interests in South Africa were not only important, they were also diverse. In 2007 UK Trade and Investment (the government agency responsible for helping British businesses abroad) listed priorities and opportunities for UK companies in water, agriculture, airports, education, power, tourism, the automotive industry, construction, healthcare, information technology and railways. Arms sales were another priority, but one which UK Trade and Investment left off the list.

Lagging a long way behind South Africa, the UK's second-most important trading partner in sub-Saharan Africa was Nigeria, where UK exports increased steadily from £535 million in 2000 to £818 million in 2005. In contrast to those in South Africa, however, the UK's business interests in Nigeria were concentrated in one sector: oil and gas. The vast bulk of UK investments in Nigeria also lay in this sector, and most of that in the form of investments by one company alone, Shell. The oil industry also accounted for the high value of UK trade and investment in Angola, which expanded considerably in the course of the 1990s and early 2000s on the back of increasing oil production. British Petroleum (BP) was the main UK player in Angola with £8 billion worth of investment planned by 2010. In 2005 UK exports to Angola (almost entirely oil-industry-related goods and services) amounted to £158 million. In the same year, UK imports from Angola amounted to around £15 million, mostly crude oil. Oil put even tiny Equatorial Guinea (with a population of little more than half a million) among the UK's more important trade partners in sub-Saharan Africa. In 2003 UK exports to Equatorial Guinea were worth £109 million, far greater than its exports to Ethiopia, the second most populous state in sub-Saharan Africa.

Elsewhere in Africa, the UK had long-standing business interests in Kenya, Ghana, Namibia, Mozambique, Tanzania, Senegal, Cameroon, Uganda and Zimbabwe. Besides BP and Shell, some of the leading UK companies operating in these countries included P&O, Land Rover, Unilever, Lonrho, British American Tobacco, Rio Tinto, Standard Chartered, Barclays, British Airways, De La Rue, Crown Agents, KPMG, Vodafone, Guinness, Cadbury, British-American Tobacco, Virgin Atlantic, BAE, Taylor Woodrow and Anglo-American. The list provides an idea of the wide range of sectors in which UK companies were involved, including defence and security, extractive industries, pharmaceuticals, banking, tourism, telecommunications and construction. Many of these companies had real clout in Whitehall, with back-channel access to the corridors of power. This was reinforced by the revolving-door phenomenon: the tendency of former special advisers, ministers and ambassadors, some of them Africa specialists, to finish off their careers with lucrative directorships or advisory jobs in the private sector.

Unlike anti-globalization campaigners, Labour's leaders saw no contradiction between helping to promote the interests of

British businesses in Africa and seeking to bring economic development, conflict resolution and poverty reduction to struggling African nations. On the contrary, even the development secretary, Clare Short, from the left of the party, believed not only that the interests of her department and British businesses overlapped but that a partnership between them was desirable. In May 1999 she told the House of Commons:

> Globalisation is creating great wealth but its benefits are unevenly spread. The growing gap between rich and poor can create instability which increases risks for us all. It is both morally right and in business' interests that this wealth is spread more fairly. Business has a key role to play in helping developing countries achieve the economic growth they need through investment and training. We are working with the private sector to promote a fair and stable operating environment necessary to achieve this. We are also working to promote socially responsible business practice.[30]

The correlation between the development interests of DfID and the business interests of major UK companies in Africa was to some extent backed up by trade and investment figures. Countries that were mired in conflict, poverty and corruption were usually countries where it was difficult for British firms to do business. UK business interests in Somalia, DR Congo and Liberia in the 1990s were non-existent or negligible. In Sudan and Zimbabwe, where the UK had a history of close business ties, increasing instability in the 1990s had led to a marked decline in UK business activities. Promoting development through resolving conflict and improving governance was therefore sometimes justified by the UK government not only as a means of reducing poverty, but also as a means of increasing the opportunities for UK business. But DfID went farther than this. Promoting business, both British and African, was to become an important part of the UK government's

45

strategy for unlocking economic growth in Africa. While UK multi-lateral and bilateral development policy encouraged privatization and public–private partnership as a mechanism for promoting economic development, UK Trade and Investment was standing by to help British companies grasp the business opportunities likely to arise from these policies.

There were also, however, contradictory interests at play between business and economic development. Corruption, poverty and conflict were not always obstacles to profit-making, especially in the extractive industries. British businesses retained or increased their investments in Nigeria and Angola through periods of dictatorship and conflict in the 1990s. When the stakes were high enough, even the most blatant and vicious corruption was not a bar to doing deals and making profits. International NGOs such as Transparency International, Human Rights Watch, Amnesty International and Global Witness were documenting clear links between the behaviour of major businesses and the poor governance, human rights abuses and violent conflicts that beset so many African states. A number of scandals, including the British 'arms to Africa' affair in Sierra Leone and a French 'arms for oil' deal with Angola, came to light which pointed in the same direction. An investigation into bribes paid by major multinational companies to secure contracts in the Lesotho Highlands Water Project led to prosecutions and fines of several 'reputable' companies. In the oil-rich Niger Delta there was evidence that the policies of oil companies were exacerbating tribal conflict and fuelling the corruption of local and national government institutions.

A Labour government with an avowedly 'ethical' foreign policy and which aimed to promote economic development, good governance and conflict prevention could not afford to ignore these well-documented links between Western business practices and poverty, corruption and conflict. To their credit the FCO and DfID did devote considerable energy, as Clare Short put it, 'to promote socially responsible business practice'. One issue that was getting a lot of attention when Labour came to power thanks to the lobbying and publicity campaigns of Global Witness and others was 'conflict diamonds' – allegations that the international diamond trade was financing conflicts in countries such as Angola and Sierra Leone. The British government took the lead in pushing for a diamond certification initiative designed to curtail the trade in conflict diamonds. This led to the creation in 2002 of the so-called Kimberley Process Certification Scheme. Its supporters claimed the scheme was an 'effective mechanism for stopping the trade in conflict diamonds'. But several years after it was launched critics said that it did not go far enough and that conflict diamonds were still finding their way on to the international market. Some also charged that the main purpose of the scheme was not to end the financing of conflicts through diamonds but to protect the de Beers diamond company, which produces 40 per cent of the world's diamonds and effectively controls the international diamond trade, from the negative fallout of the controversy over conflict diamonds.

Other UK-backed schemes to promote corporate social responsibility included: the Extractive Industries Transparency Initiative, which encouraged governments and companies to publish their payments and revenues as a means of ensuring greater accountability in the oil, gas and mining sectors; the implementation of the OECD guidelines for multinational enterprises, which aimed to set higher standards of responsible business conduct in areas such as employment, human rights, environment and accountability; the Ethical Trading Initiative, which aims to promote adherence to international labour standards along companies' international supply chains; and the UN Global Compact. Such initiatives were more than just window dressing. Together with the NGO lobbying that gave rise to them, they did help to increase the sensitivity of companies to the links between their activities and corruption, conflict, environmental degradation, exploitation of workers' rights and other abuses. Large companies whose profitability depended on maintaining good reputations were particularly sensitive. But ultimately the voluntary nature of all these schemes limited their effectiveness as a means of bringing about substantive changes in corporate behaviour on the ground, especially in those unstable parts of Africa where a change of practice was most urgent. And calls for mandatory regulation went unheeded by government and business alike on the grounds that such regulation was unrealistic, unenforceable and would reduce the competitiveness of 'reputable' businesses, leaving the field open to less scrupulous operators.

As the business-friendly Labour government developed its policies towards Africa it had to square its development aims not only with the interests of major UK firms doing business in Africa but also with those of UK businesses at home. Increasingly DfID and other players in Whitehall came to see reducing trade barriers to African exports as an important component of a successful development strategy. But here the government's advocates of African development through trade had to contend with the business and farming lobbies in the UK and in the wider European Union who were not willing to give up their competitive edge by lowering tariffs on imports. Year after year there was an ever-widening gap between the noble rhetoric of Western politicians on the links between trade and development and the reality of what their governments were actually pushing for on behalf of domestic farming and manufacturing interests in world trade negotiations.

Gunboat development

Blair's 'doctrine of international community' articulated in Chicago in 1999 had some startling implications for the Ministry of Defence, especially in the light of the difficulties the British armed forces had experienced in Bosnia and Northern Ireland. Was the military prepared for humanitarian interventions of the kind envisaged by Blair's Chicago speech? How many interventions would it be called upon to implement at any one time? Where would the troops and equipment come from, and would they prove to be fit for purpose? How could one define victory in such wars? Would the politicians provide political strategies for success and all the resources that would be required to undertake post-conflict reconstruction, national reconciliation and state-building? Or would the military be left in open-ended deployments with no obvious exit strategies?

The end of the cold war had raised a lot of questions about the need for new military doctrines and postures. By 1997 the British armed forces had experienced a new kind of conflict in Bosnia and were still digesting its lessons. A decade on there were still as many questions as answers. The challenge of adapting to the changing security environment was not made any easier after 9/11 when the British military was called upon to perform in several new theatres, each presenting a very distinct and difficult set of operational, political and developmental challenges. Operating at the sharp end of Blair's foreign policies in the Balkans, in Sierra Leone and later in Afghanistan and Iraq, the MoD encountered both successes and failures. But by 2007 it was suffering a severe case of overstretch, fighting open-ended conflicts in both Afghanistan and Iraq. The strain was beginning to tell. Morale was low and retired generals were complaining vociferously that the armed forces were being given tasks that they were not equipped to perform.

It is not just that the military has been materially ill equipped to fight the 'new wars'. Britain's politicians have also been ideologically and intellectually ill equipped for them. The nub of it is that in all these campaigns, with the partial exception of

Sierra Leone, Britain and its allies have been missing a crucial ingredient for overall victory in these kinds of conflicts: political strategy. As General Sir Rupert Smith, one of the UK's most experienced military commanders, has pointed out, today's wars are wars fought among people rather than between states.[31] They are wars of persuasion rather than wars of survival. At the tactical level the MoD, taking advantage of its experiences in Northern Ireland, has adapted its posture and doctrines to the requirements of peacekeeping and counter-insurgency. But in Afghanistan and Iraq, British and American political leaders, convinced by their own rhetoric that these are in fact wars of survival, were still using the doctrine of all-out industrial war – a doctrine that basically aims at 'victory at all costs'. But in these kinds of conflict the overweening use of force is counterproductive. What is required is not Churchillian 'victory at all costs' but victory in the more subtle battle of wills, the struggle to win hearts and minds. What is required is a political strategy to win the people over, to reconcile warring factions and to rebuild and in some cases reconfigure nations. The all-important ingredients of success are political negotiation and a willingness to compromise and even to appease the enemy – all things that Blair and his American ally explicitly ruled out in these conflicts.

In Africa in 1997 it was clear that any effective international action to address the problems of the continent would require a military component. But the experiences of the Americans and the UN in Somalia, the French in Rwanda and the West African peacekeeping force in Liberia and Sierra Leone all gave pause for serious thought. All these interventions had failed, and they had mainly failed because of the lack of a political strategy for success. These failures foreshadowed the essential deficit of the strategic approach in the later interventions in Afghanistan and Iraq. From a military and tactical point of view the military interventions in Africa in the 1990s demonstrated that political understanding

of the context and history of the conflicts was just as important as military capability, that good intelligence, linguists and
anthropologists were just as important as boots on the ground.
To win hearts and minds, it is essential to understand what local
people are saying and thinking and, crucially, what they think
of you. In Somalia in 1993/94, the Americans got sucked into
a conflict they did not understand and could not control and
became more part of the problem than facilitators of a solution.
UN forces got bogged down in conflicts from Somalia to Sierra
Leone and DR Congo for similar reasons. At the strategic level
what was needed to make these interventions work was a political
strategy that brought together the military, diplomatic and economic components in a coherent whole, taking into account not
only the national dynamics of the conflict but also the regional
ones. This required patience, resources and political will. It also
required flexibility, imagination and innovation. In the 1990s,
African crises just didn't seem worth it. Today the West expresses
surprise, guilt and shame that there was no Western military
intervention in Rwanda in 1994. In fact at the time few thought
that an intervention in a remote and little-known African country
was feasible or wise. So soon after the failure of the intervention
in Somalia in 1993 it was inevitable that the West should think
twice about another one to stop the Rwandan genocide.

Bearing the recent examples of failed military operations in
mind, the British military establishment was hesitant about
committing forces to Sierra Leone in 2000 and overcame its
reluctance only when Whitehall came up with a coherent and
costly political and economic plan in support of the military operation. As it turned out, circumstances were favourable in Sierra
Leone. The rebels were ill equipped and poorly trained. Many of
them were traumatized children. They had made themselves so
unpopular by their brutal tactics against civilians that the task
of winning hearts and minds was not difficult. Furthermore it

was a small country and the conflict there was relatively simple compared to the conflicts in DR Congo or Somalia (or Iraq and Afghanistan). With the right mix of military and policing tactics the UK's exercise in gunboat development in Sierra Leone succeeded. As for the long-term political strategy, the creation of an effective independent state capable of delivering security and economic development to its citizens, that is still incomplete seven years after the British intervention, in spite of what is the largest per capita injection of UK overseas development assistance into any country in the world.

After 11 September 2001 the British armed forces' attention and resources were diverted from Africa to Afghanistan and Iraq and there was no appetite for further military operations in Africa. When called upon to support a French-led EU force in Bunia in eastern DR Congo in 2003, the MoD refused to provide more than a token presence. The large-scale and costly commitment to Iraq and Afghanistan ruled out any serious consideration of significant British involvement in military efforts to address the crisis in Darfur. Instead the British military presence in Africa was limited to its programme of training African peacekeepers; the provision of military advisers and logistical support to African and UN peacekeeping operations; advising and training selected African allies such as South Africa and Nigeria; and liaising with the US military's growing counterterrorism operations on the continent. The demands made by the prime minister on British forces in Afghanistan and Iraq in the unfolding US-led, UK-supported 'war on terrorism' meant that after Sierra Leone the British armed forces were unable to offer any serious military help on the continent where they had achieved their greatest success.

2 | The policy

'From the very beginning I wanted to forge a new partnership with African leaders and countries. Not based on rich and poor or donor and recipient but based on common values of justice, democracy and human rights; a partnership of trust and equality.' Tony Blair, speech in South Africa, 31 May 2007

On 7 July 2005, Tony Blair was hosting a G8 summit in Gleneagles in Scotland which he hoped would secure sincere commitment from the world's richest nations to step up their assistance to Africa. When news of bomb attacks in central London came through Blair rushed to the city to help deal with the crisis. It looked as though the summit's efforts on Africa would be over-shadowed by the attacks. To some extent they were. But in his characteristically nimble way Blair was able, on his return to Gleneagles to wrap up the summit, to make a powerful point, contrasting the destructiveness of the terrorist attacks with what he was trying to achieve on Africa.

The $50 billion uplift in aid, the signal for a new deal on trade, the cancellation of the debts of the poorest nations, universal access to Aids treatment, the commitment to a new peace-keeping force for Africa, the commitment in return by Africa's leaders to democracy, and good governance, and the rule of law. All of this does not change the world tomorrow, it is a beginning, not an end, and none of it today will match the same ghastly impact as the cruelty of terror. But it has a pride, and a hope, and a humanity at its heart that can lift the shadow of terrorism and light the way to a better future.[1]

This was heady and stirring stuff, a fascinating combination of policy and poetry. There was little room for doubt about the morality of the message. But how far would the UK be able to deliver on the promises of its missionary prime minister?

The 2005 summit in Gleneagles was an important culmination of the UK's policy in Africa under Labour. Spurred on by the success of Sierra Leone, Blair had made Africa an explicit priority for his second term in office. By 2001 a reasonably coherent set of British government policies on Africa had come into view. These emerged from the influences and interests that were driving the main Whitehall players, and crucially from the government's reaction to events on the ground. Four main elements of the UK policy stand out: the idea of 'enhanced partnership' with African governments committed to good governance, conflict prevention and poverty reduction; the big push for a massive increase in aid, debt relief, trade and investment as the primary means of stimulating economic development; the deliberate effort to strengthen the UK's international networking and relations with state and non-state actors, including international celebrities, as a crucial means of increasing the UK's leverage to effect change in Africa; and the continuing importance of protecting and promoting the UK's national interests in Africa.

The first two elements of the policy were inextricably linked: unless African governments were committed to both the political and economic fundamentals of development there could be no justification for a push for increased assistance from the donors. I explore the UK's approach to the politics and economics of development in the first three sections of this chapter. The first section looks at the UK's search for African partners, and focuses in particular on the UK's role in supporting the emergence of the New Partnership for African Development (NEPAD) and the African Union (AU). Here the UK hoped to solve an important part of the development conundrum by creating a mechanism for 'enhanced partnership' between the donors and African governments that were committed to good governance and poverty reduction. The second section explores the UK's across-the-board approach to improved governance, conflict prevention, 'human development', aid, debt relief, trade and investment. This section focuses mainly on the report of Blair's Commission for Africa, published in March 2005, which represents the clearest comprehensive statement of the UK's policy on development in Africa. The third section highlights the failure of UK development policy to provide satisfactory answers to crucial questions about governance, politics and culture in Africa.

Although economic development, poverty reduction, conflict prevention and good governance were what the UK displayed most prominently in the shop window of its Africa policy, London had other interests and priorities in Africa on behalf of which it was bound to act. In the fourth section of this chapter I examine some of the objectives of the UK in Africa in relation to the most crucial of these interests: counterterrorism, energy security, commerce, migration and climate change. In the fifth and final section of the chapter I examine the partnerships and relationships with other external actors, including international celebrities, which the UK cultivated in pursuit of its range of policy objectives in Africa.

Partners for development

By 2000 a new crop of leaders had come to power in Africa who seemed to be more committed to good governance, conflict management and poverty reduction than their predecessors. Among those who stood out were Thabo Mbeki, who became president of South Africa in 1999, Ghana's John Kufuor, elected to succeed the former military dictator Jerry Rawlings in 2000, Senegal's Abdoulaye Wade, who also came to power in 2000, Olusegun Obasanjo, a former military ruler who was elected in 1999 to be Nigeria's first civilian leader in sixteen years, and Tanzania's Benjamin Mkapa, who had been elected in 1995 in the country's first multi-party elections. Clare Short had also cultivated another group of longer-serving African heads of state who had less impressive democratic credentials and who had all arrived in power by force of arms but who appealed to Short's left-wing politics: Rwanda's Paul Kagame, Uganda's Yoweri Museveni and Ethiopia's Meles Zenawi. All three were beginning to receive increasing amounts of UK economic aid.

In discussions with Mbeki and others between 1999 and 2000, Blair hit upon the idea of a mechanism that would demonstrate to African governments that if they signed up to and made concrete steps towards implementing a donor-approved vision of economic development and poverty reduction based on better governance and progress on resolving conflicts, then the donors would come in behind such governments with more aid, debt relief, access to international markets and investment. Such a mechanism, it was hoped, would not only reward those who were deemed to be performing well, but would also soon encourage poor performers to clean up their acts and set their countries on the path to sound economic and political development. The UK worked for months with African governments and with its international partners try-ing to make the concept work. Blair himself invested considerable energy in the project, meeting with African leaders to push it in the direction he wanted it to go. So committed was he to the idea that one of the few engagements in his diary that was not cancelled in the days after 11 September 2001 was a meeting with selected African leaders at his Chequers country home.

In spite of the effort, however, what emerged at the end of the process was a watered-down compromise very different from Blair's original idea. Blair had not counted on African politics. Zimbabwe and Libya were painted by the UK government as the main saboteurs of Blair's NEPAD concept. In fact it was more complicated than that. First, there was an unspoken rule among African leaders that however much rivalry there was among them in private, in public – and especially in their public dealings with the rest of the world – they tended towards solidarity. Second, African leaders were fiercely reluctant to be put in a position where they could be portrayed as doing the work of outsiders, especially an outsider like the UK with its long colonial past in Africa. Third, there was the usual rivalry between anglophones and francophones, with Senegal's Wade, supported by France, pushing for a rival vision of African economic development and partnership through his 'Omega Plan', which he insisted should be incorporated into the final agreement. Finally most African leaders, whether of the old school or the new, and whether committed to good governance or not, wanted to elaborate their own development plans, not have them designed for them and imposed on them by foreigners. This is something that Clare Short understood very well, but Blair didn't.

What emerged in the end was a continent-wide programme in which the idea of an enhanced partnership with good performers was all but lost. In the end, the only really innovative aspects of NEPAD were a rhetorical acknowledgement of the complementary responsibilities of African governments and donors (Africans to improve their own governance, donors to increase their financial support) and an Africa Peer Review Mechanism by which African states were supposed to measure each other's performance according to a set of agreed benchmarks of good governance. But for those Africans who were not committed to better governance the rhetoric of NEPAD remained rhetoric. As for the Africa Peer Review Mechanism, that never really got off the ground, in spite of considerable financial and technical support from the UK. NEPAD's first big test was Zimbabwe, where the crisis was escalating just at the time when NEPAD was coming into existence. It failed the test dismally. Most of the African leaders involved in NEPAD refused even to raise their voices in support of the victims of Robert Mugabe's attacks on democracy in Zimbabwe, let alone criticize Mugabe himself or take any serious diplomatic action against him.

The emergence of NEPAD went hand in hand with the inauguration in 2001 of the AU to replace the discredited Organization of African Unity (OAU), the old talking shop for African dictators. This was another African initiative that received strong support from the UK, even though the inclusive nature of the AU made it a flimsy tool for promoting the concept of 'enhanced partnership' between donors and good performers. Like NEPAD, the AU (which later adopted NEPAD as one of its key programmes) sought to draw a line under the old style of African politics. The AU dispensed with the OAU principle of non-interference of African states in each other's affairs (honoured as much in the breach as in the observance) and replaced it with the principle of non-indifference to internal conflicts and abuses carried out by African states against their citizens. In, too, came commitments to promoting conflict resolution, democracy, human rights, good governance and economic integration, as well as pan-African mechanisms to implement these commitments, such as the Peace and Security Council, an African parliament and eventually a host of other institutions, including an African central bank, a court of justice and a commission on human and peoples' rights. For all the rhetoric surrounding the new approach of the revamped African body and its supposed 'non-indifference' to the internal affairs of African states, the AU, like NEPAD, failed to take a strong position on the one African issue of the day which really mattered to the UK: Zimbabwe. But, as the FCO understood better than Blair, this was inevitable. The UK's own failed diplomacy on Zimbabwe had played into Mugabe's hands and made it much more difficult for African states to criticize Mugabe, let alone manage the Zimbabwe crisis.

In fact in its first few years the AU did take some principled positions on African crises. Not only that, but it also soon proved its worth to the donors, including the UK, by demonstrating its willingness to engage in conflict management and peacekeeping. The donors were already spending large amounts of money on UN peacekeeping operations in Africa and were having a lot of difficulty in finding troops to fill them. The AU's new readiness to deploy peacekeepers offered a cut-price alternative. Within five years of its creation the AU had deployed peacekeeping operations to Burundi, Darfur and Somalia. Soon the donors, principally the EU, were channelling most of their assistance to the AU into paying for these operations and building African capacity to deploy them.

It soon became clear, however, that the AU and NEPAD were insufficiently strong foundations on which to build mechanisms for 'enhanced partnership' between donors and African governments. But Blair was not deterred by this or by the meagre results of his efforts. Far from it, he pressed determinedly ahead with his support for NEPAD and the AU and argued to sceptical allies (and officials within his own government) that they were sufficient bases on which to proceed with a massive increase in donor support to Africa. From 2001 onwards the prime minister ran tenaciously with this ball, insisting that Africa be placed prominently on the agenda of the annual set-piece summits of the Group of Eight industrialized nations (G8) and lobbying the Americans, Canadians, Europeans and Japanese to commit more and more assistance to the cause of economic development in Africa. Not even the events of 11 September 2001 deterred him. On the contrary, they convinced him that rescuing Africa from poverty and conflict was more urgent than ever.

While Blair was pulling out the stops to persuade the other rich countries to put their money behind his Africa gamble in a great exercise of multilateral leverage, on a bilateral basis DfID was quietly operating its own policy of 'enhanced partnership' with African states it believed were committed to good governance, poverty reduction and conflict prevention. The implementation of this policy is explored more fully in the next chapter. But it is important to note here that DfID's thinking and practice on development by now represented a radical and bold, if risky, new departure. The main innovation was a switch from delivering aid in a highly controlling manner through programmes managed (often very inefficiently) by development agencies and NGOs to direct budget support. This entailed a UK commitment to regular direct transfers of substantial financial assistance over a relatively long term. Those selected as favoured 'partners' were African governments that DfID felt were committed to good governance and poverty reduction and which had in place sufficient budgetary oversight to provide accountability for how the money was spent. The policy recognized that good governance was the key to good development and made the calculation that even in the difficult circumstances of a Rwanda or an Ethiopia, putting long-term funding into the hands of governments that had worked out their own development and poverty reduction strategies was the most effective way of reducing poverty and stimulating economic development. By 2005 DfID was channelling direct budget support to seventeen African countries. But the policy of 'enhanced partnership' which DfID pursued bilaterally raised important questions. How did one measure commitment, and what if the countries selected for enhanced partnership turned out not to be as committed to good governance and poverty reduction as DfID supposed? What of the many African states that clearly were not committed to good governance or poverty reduction but which also desperately needed development assistance? And was aid the most effective way of achieving economic development anyway?

A 'blisteringly honest' report

In March 2004, a year into the Iraq war, Blair established a Commission for Africa to look at the economics and politics of development and come up with a coherent plan for African regeneration ahead of the 2005 summit in Gleneagles. In keeping with his policy of using celebrity for political ends, Blair made the Irish anti-poverty campaigner and rock singer Bob Geldof (who had suggested the idea of a Commission in the first place) a member of the Commission and relied on him to publicize it. The Commission's mandate was 'to define the challenges facing Africa, and to provide clear recommendations on how to support the changes needed to reduce poverty'.[2] The Commission for Africa's 461-page report was published in March 2005 under the title *Our Common Interest*. In keeping with London's view that partnership with Africa was an essential component of any successful policy, the Commission included a majority of African members – including two serving African rulers, Meles Zenawi of Ethiopia and Benjamin Mkapa of Tanzania, as well as the influential South African finance minister, Trevor Manuel. Furthermore the Commission was at pains to demonstrate the extent to which, in drawing up its report, it had consulted with a wide range of African opinion.

Much of this was cosmetic, however. In fact the report of the Commission for Africa was an entirely UK-driven and -controlled initiative, and as such it was not particularly well received either in African political circles or by the other donors. Even within the UK government, the Commission for Africa was a source of friction. On the one hand it became another arena for the personal animosity between Blair and Gordon Brown, both of whom were represented on the Commission. On the other hand it aggravated relations between DfID and the FCO. The new Secretary for International Development, Hilary Benn (who had taken over at DfID a few months after the resignation of Clare

Short over the war in Iraq), was represented on the Commission. But the FCO was almost entirely excluded. Not only was the Foreign Secretary, Jack Straw, not represented on the Commission, but the FCO was not even consulted on its composition. And Myles Wickstead, the former ambassador to Ethiopia who was appointed as the head of the Commission Secretariat, was sidelined after the Chancellor, Gordon Brown, seconded one of his top economic advisers, Nicholas Stern, from the Treasury to be the Commission's director of policy and research. Stern effectively drafted the whole report and tailored it to the political needs of the UK government.

Part moral exhortation, part argument and analysis and part blueprint, the report of the Commission for Africa comes closer to a comprehensive overview of the UK's approach to the politics and economics of development in Africa than any other single statement produced by the Labour government between 1997 and 2007. As such, even though the report itself was quickly shelved and the process that produced it soon forgotten, it contains much useful and clearly expressed substance on policy. The first thing that strikes the reader about the report is that, like many of Blair's own statements on Africa, it is permeated with a passionate, sometimes strident, morality. In their very first sentences the commissioners set the tone.

> The world is awash with wealth, and on a scale which has never been seen before in human history … Yet it is not a wealth which everyone enjoys. In Africa millions of people live each day in abject poverty and squalor. Children are hungry, their bodies deformed and stunted by malnutrition. They cannot read or write. They are needlessly ill. They have to drink dirty water. Those living in Africa's mushrooming shanty towns live by stinking rubbish tips and breathe polluted air … There is a tsunami every month in Africa. But its deadly tide of disease and hunger

steals silently and secretly across the continent ... Its victims die quietly, out of sight, hidden in their pitiful homes. But they perish in the same numbers. The eyes of the world may be averted from their routine suffering, but the eyes of history are upon us. In years to come, future generations will look back, and wonder how could our world have known and failed to act? ... The time is ripe for change. That is the conviction of us all. Acting together we have the power to shape history. To do nothing would be intolerable. To do something is not enough. To do everything we can is not only a requirement, it is our clear duty. Now is the time to act.[3]

The wording and the style suggested that the Commission for Africa's report was meant to shock and shame its readers into action. But this approach immediately raised a number of questions. First, the strategy was clearly designed to make the rich dig into their pockets for charity. And the thrust of the report, as we shall see, was to argue that what the rich countries of the world needed above all to do for Africa was to give it more money. But was this really the answer to Africa's problems? After all, even the Commission for Africa acknowledged that what Africa needed above all was better government. Second, the report's argument effectively made Africa's destiny dependent on the charity proffered by the rich world and therefore raised the question of what would happen if the rich world suddenly went into economic decline owing to dwindling energy resources or found it had greater priorities for its overseas spending, for example in securing the Middle East or fighting terrorism. And a third question was this: what if it turned out that, even though Africa's underdevelopment presented a threat to the rich world, its economic development actually turned out to present an even greater threat to the rich world? It was after all at least imaginable that Africa's economic development would put even greater pressure on the world's energy supplies, exacerbate the problem of global warming and, through education, increase the potential for Africans to turn to anti-Western radicalism.

None of these awkward questions seems to have disturbed the tranquillity of the drafters of the report as they surveyed the problems of Africa and the continent's relations with the rest of the world. It was simply assumed that more aid was the key component of the solution to Africa's poverty, that the industrialized world would maintain its economic stability, or grow richer, and that both the donors and Africa would benefit equally from Africa's economic development.

In fact, in presenting its rationale for greater economic assistance to Africa from rich nations the report was at pains to use the quintessentially 'third way' argument that it was in the interests of the rich to help reduce poverty in Africa. As we have already seen, this was an argument that DfID and the FCO had already developed, and the Commission for Africa took it a step farther.

> A stable and growing Africa will provide a market of several hundred million people into which the rest of the world can sell its goods and services ... It will also provide a stable source of supplies. Africa holds seven per cent of world oil reserves ... By 2015 Africa will provide 25 per cent of the oil imports into the United States.[4]

If on the other hand Africa failed to grow and develop, the report maintained, this would be 'bad for the rest of the world'. Migration, disease and international terrorism and crime were identified as the now familiar menaces that the rich world would face if it failed to cough up to help Africa.

But other arguments were offered too. The report reasoned that if Africa's problems were not addressed now Africa would not simply struggle on in its current state. The problems would get bigger and more difficult to solve. There would be deeper levels of poverty, conflicts would spread and become more violent and virulent, and irreversible damage would be done to the environment. Furthermore, the 'reformers' who were lining up to engage with the donors on a big push for African development and were committing to honour their half of the bargain (to tackle corruption and conflicts) needed to deliver economic development to their citizens – otherwise they would be kicked out of office by less cooperative, less 'moderate' political forces, including populists and religious extremists. And finally the report argued that with the help of foreign aid, technical assistance and political backing many African states were already making significant progress in tackling poverty, improving economic growth, resolving armed conflicts, and reducing corruption. 'All is not gloom,' the report stated right at the outset. Change was afoot in Africa. Governments were 'showing a new vision ... Africa, at last, looks set to deliver'.[5] There existed, in the opinion of the commissioners, an important opportunity to build on positive economic and political trends in Africa to lift the continent out of its predicament.

Obviously this last claim risked undermining the force of the moral argument for action. If things were already improving, then why was there such an urgent need for action? One answer was that things were not improving fast enough. But the Commission for Africa also needed to be able to identify some improvement in order to justify the main remedy it was proposing for Africa's ills: a massive increase in foreign assistance. Given that Africa was already receiving very high levels of foreign aid, the Commission would seriously undermine the argument for the additional aid if it turned out that all that had gone before had been a waste of money, with no concrete improvements to show for it. Thus, at the risk of inconsistency, it was necessary to add hope to the emotions of shame, greed and fear that the Commission was counting on as spurs to persuade the rich to do more to assist the world's poorest continent.

The Commission for Africa's report prided itself on being a

'blisteringly honest' account of Africa's past and present. And indeed the report did not shy away from many important truths or from identifying most of the internal and external sources of Africa's ills. The failure of African states to deliver security and economic and social development to their populations lay at the heart of the analysis of the Commission for Africa's report. If states could be fixed so that they 'functioned' properly in terms of delivering basic services and security, then all would be well. Fixing African states, according to the report, required action in four major areas, all of them interlinked: governance, conflict prevention, human development and poverty reduction.

On governance the report was refreshingly hard hitting. 'Africa', the report stated, 'has suffered from governments that have looted the resources of the state; that could not or would not deliver services to their people; that in many cases were predatory, corruptly extracting their countries' resources; that maintained control through violence and bribery; and that squandered or stole aid.'[6] The report accused the external donors of having turned a blind eye to the governance shortcomings of their African allies, but suggested charitably that this was essentially a cold war failing that no longer applied. It was therefore now up to the Africans themselves, the report said, to change the behaviour of their governments. And the more successful they were in this endeavour, 'the greater the effectiveness of external support'.[7] This was the closest the report came to saying that unless African states became more accountable and more democratic then giving them more aid or cancelling their debts would not work. But the report quickly moved to qualify the statement by saying that 'external support can also work to foster such change'. What the report did not address was the fact that external support could also do precisely the opposite. This was a clear lesson from much of the continent in the 1980s. But even now there was little evidence that foreign aid was helping

Sudan, Ethiopia, Nigeria, Rwanda or Sierra Leone to become more accountable and democratic.

In order to address the 'governance deficit' in Africa, the Commission for Africa, closely reflecting the UK's policy that was soon to be laid out in a DfID White Paper,[8] proposed a two-pronged approach aimed at building both the capacity and the accountability of African states. The specific measures recommended were mostly technical rather than political, and they included: providing strong support for pan-African and regional organizations, particularly the AU and NEPAD; persuading donors to support comprehensive national strategies for capacity-building; building up professional skills and knowledge, e.g. by revitalizing Africa's higher education; broadening participation and strengthening institutions that improve accountability, including parliaments, local authorities, the media and the justice system; increasing the transparency of revenues and budgets, especially in countries rich in natural resources; and tackling corruption, 'including repatriation of stolen state assets'.

The second problem requiring urgent attention was armed civil conflict. This was self-evident from the recent history of Africa. But there was little reflection in the report on the possibility that conflict, even violent conflict, though in many ways destructive and harmful, could also be part of a process of political transformation, not all of it negative, and that in turning to armed conflict some Africans were, often as a last resort, responding to intolerable discrimination or seeking to achieve justice. Given that the UK itself had already several times turned to violence as a means of securing political objectives under the Labour government, including in Africa, this seemed a curious omission.

The Commission's answer to the problem of armed conflict in Africa, and here again the recommendations were lifted straight from the conflict management policies for Africa developed by the UK government over the previous half-decade, was a big increase in investment by the donors in the conflict prevention capacity of African states and regional organizations. Specifically the Commission for Africa had in mind: 'building the capacity of African states and society to prevent and manage conflict by tackling its root causes'. This included 'steps to make aid more effective at building the foundations for durable peace, to improve the management of natural resource revenues, and to tackle the trade in small arms' and conflicts over resources. Another major recommendation was to strengthen the ability of African regional organizations and the UN to prevent and resolve conflict through, for example, more effective early warning, mediation and peace-keeping. The Commission also proposed that donors provide 'flexible funding for African Union and regional organizations' core [peacekeeping] capacity and operations' and called for better coordination and greater funding for post-conflict reconstruction, 'so that states emerging from violent conflict do not slide back into it'.[9]

The third area identified as a priority for the world's attention was what the Commission called 'human development', by which it mainly meant improvements in health, hygiene and education. According to the Commission's analysis, lack of investment in human development is not only a consequence of the dysfunction of African states but also a cause of it. The report described a vicious circle in which states that failed to deliver adequate education, health and hygiene services to their populations were setting themselves up for further weakness and failure because a sick and uneducated population is a social liability which itself undermines a state's economic prospects as well as its stability, and ultimately its political viability: 'The challenges are immense. If we continue as we are, the Millennium Development Goals (MDGs) for halving poverty, for universal primary education and for the elimination of avoidable infant deaths in sub-Saharan

Africa will not be delivered in 2015 but between 100 and 150 years late.'[10]

The Commission's analysis of failings in tackling human development in Africa highlighted in particular the challenge of HIV, which in 2004 'killed over two million people in sub-Saharan Africa with more than three million infected in that year alone'. The analysis of the human development failures in Africa also took donors to task for failing to provide the right kind of funding for health and education. Donor support in these areas had been 'short term, volatile and largely tied to using people and products from donor countries'.[11] But nowhere was there any reflection that aid itself, not the way it was delivered, might be part of the problem. Instead the Commission simply proposed throwing more and better aid at the problems of 'human development' in order to achieve measurable outcomes such as free education and free basic healthcare for all, improving sanitation and access to clean water, and dramatically reducing the prevalence of HIV.

Like the British government, the Commission for Africa saw its main objective as poverty reduction, and like the British government it identified economic growth as the best means of achieving this objective. But what was the best way to boost economic growth? Improving 'governance', resolving conflicts and investing in health and education were important ingredients. But they were not enough. Economic performance, according to the Commission's report, had improved across much of Africa in the last decade, but not enough in most countries to prevent continuing increases in levels of poverty in most African countries. The Commission said it was necessary to increase the average growth rate of African states to 7 per cent by 2010 and to sustain such growth thereafter. To do this it would be necessary for donors to invest heavily in infrastructure; to work with the public and private sectors to remove the obstacles to investment; and to release 'Africa's entrepreneurial energies' by facilitating better access to markets, finance and business linkages. All this, of course, needed to be achieved in an 'environmentally sustainable' way.[12]

The Commission for Africa's programme, signed up to by the UK's prime minister, Chancellor of the Exchequer and international development secretary, was going to cost a lot of money. Only a fraction of it was going to come from the UK's own development budget. So where was the rest going to come from? This was a question that the Commission for Africa set itself to address with energy and in meticulous detail. What would unlock the needed resources for African development, according to the Commission, were three things: more and fairer trade with the rest of the world, more and better aid from the donors, and debt cancellation.

On trade the Commission's report proposed, first, improving Africa's capacity to trade by addressing Africa's familiar governance and security problems, removing Africa's own internal trade barriers and investing heavily in creating a favourable environment in which Africans could produce and trade efficiently and competitively. Customs reform and investment in trading infrastructure (ports, roads and telecommunications) are of course an important part of this. Second, it was essential to improve Africa's access to the markets of the rich world. To do this the report recommended a highly ambitious programme for world trade negotiations, including: immediate agreement on the part of rich nations to eliminate their trade-distorting support to their own cotton and sugar producing sectors; commitment to ending all their export subsidies by 2010; and agreement to reduce all their trade tariffs on African imports to zero by 2015. In addition the report sought commitment from higher-income developing countries to reduce their trade barriers to African exporters.[13]

On aid the report recommended a doubling of foreign aid levels between 2005 and 2010. This would be achieved through a combination of factors. First donors would have to meet their existing commitments to move towards the target of overseas development assistance at a rate of 0.7 per cent of gross national income. Second, finance would need to be raised in capital markets though an International Finance Facility which would front-load aid on the strength of future aid commitments already made by donors (i.e. the donors would borrow in order to raise funds for development); and international levies (for example, a tax on airline tickets) would be raised with revenues dedicated to development. Not only should the quantity of aid be increased, its quality also needed to be improved. This would be achieved, according to the Commission for Africa, by among other things

> strengthening the processes of accountability to citizens in aid-recipient countries; allocating aid to countries where poverty is deepest and where aid can be best used; providing much stronger support to advancing governance where conditions for effective use of aid are currently weak; channelling more aid through grants, to avoid the build-up of debt; aligning more closely with country priorities, procedures, systems, and practices; providing aid more predictably and flexibly over the longer term; protecting countries better against unanticipated shocks.[14]

The crucial contradiction latent in these recommendations was this: it was impossible to secure the accountability of African governments without undermining African 'ownership', but it was impossible to give away 'ownership' without compromising accountability and good governance. Nowhere did the report address this dilemma.

On debt the report was equally ambitious in its proposal, no doubt relying on the support for debt cancellation generated by the campaigning of Geldof, fellow rock star Bono and the humanitarian NGOs. The report urged:

> For poor countries in sub-Saharan Africa which need it, the objective must be 100 per cent debt cancellation as soon as

possible ... The key criterion should be that the money be used to deliver development, economic growth and the reduction of poverty for countries actively promoting good governance.[15]

Like so much of the advocacy on debt cancellation, this formulation risked putting the cart before the horse. The poor countries that needed debt relief the most were not poor primarily because of their debt but because of bad government (and bad donor policies) of which the massive debts were simply a manifestation. But as long as bad government continued there was very little chance that the money released by debt cancellation would be seriously channelled into economic growth, poverty reduction and the promotion of good governance. In 2005 the Paris Club cancelled $18 billion of Nigeria's $30 billion debt on the grounds that it was making impressive progress on economic reform. In the same year Transparency International listed Nigeria as one of the ten most corrupt countries in the world. In 2007 the UK-backed ruling party that had made such impressive progress stayed on in power after elections that were widely seen as among the most blatantly rigged in Nigeria's history.

The headlines of the Commission for Africa's report were preordained: aid and debt relief with specific numbers attached to each. Government advisers on development knew that trade and investment were probably more important ingredients of successful economic development in Africa, but they also knew that it would be much more difficult to secure pledges from the donors on trade and investment than on aid and debt. And so aid and debt relief were pushed to the top of the Commission's agenda and became the big story of Gleneagles. In this sense the Commission's report was less than 'blisteringly honest'. Two years on from Gleneagles even the pledges that Blair extracted from the G8 on aid and debt were still billions of dollars away from being met. Progress on trade and investment (which the UK recognized as crucial ingredients of successful development) were nowhere to be seen. Brown's efforts to secure funds for investment in African development from capital markets through the International Finance Facility had not borne fruit. The so-called Doha development round of World Trade Organization negotiations were not going in Africa's direction. At the G8 summit in Germany in 2007 anti-poverty campaigners felt they had been conned by the hype of Gleneagles. The pop singer Bono, who had contributed to the hype, said he felt misled: 'I might be a rock star, but I can count.'[16]

But arguably a much bigger question than the glaring gap between rhetoric and reality on aid, debt, trade and investment was the question of the coherence of the Commission for Africa's argument, and by extension of the UK's policy towards Africa. Undoubtedly the report (and subsequent UK pronouncements on governance) made the case that the central obstacle to Africa's development was poor governance – i.e. bad government. But although it could obviously point to examples where aid had made a difference in improving education or healthcare, it signally failed to make even a theoretical case that more aid would help rather than hinder the achievement of better governance. Indeed, on this central issue there is just one short paragraph in the whole 461-page report:

> Recent research finds that aid of the right type and timing substantially increases the chances that a country will achieve a sustained turnaround from weak institutions and governance. With carefully designed technical assistance and the provision of post-primary education, it is possible for aid to improve the institutional environment. One example of this gradual process of turnaround assisted by appropriate aid is Ghana, which has evolved from a coup-ridden country to a democracy that is sustaining growth. Another example is the turnaround in Ethiopia during the past decade.[17]

This is hardly a cast-iron case. Almost before the ink was dry on the report, events in Ethiopia were to show that the 'turnaround' in that country was illusory. In May 2005, Meles Zenawi, the most prominent African on the Commission, ordered a violent clampdown on the Ethiopian opposition in the aftermath of a disputed and quite blatantly rigged election. Almost two hundred demonstrators were killed, some of them shot dead by police marksmen on the streets of Addis Ababa, thousands of opposition supporters were detained and seventy-six political activists, including the leaders of the main opposition party, were arrested and charged with capital offences including treason and outrage of the constitution. There could be no better illustration of the failure of Britain's policy towards Africa to take into account the all-important political context in which it was supposed to be implemented.

Politics as culture

The closest the Commission came to an analysis of the complex political dimensions of aid and of Africa's relationship with donors was a chapter on 'culture' entitled 'Through African Eyes'.[18] Of all the chapters in the Commission for Africa's report, this one seemed the farthest removed from British government policy; indeed, it contained within it, albeit in an oblique and undeveloped form, devastating criticism of the UK approach to African development as articulated under the Labour government.

The chapter starts with a warning and an example. The warning is that 'ideas and actions not premised on African culture would not work'. The example is from Somaliland, the breakaway self-declared (but internationally unrecognized) state in north-western Somalia which was the only part of that country which regained a semblance of statehood and political stability in the aftermath of the collapse of the central government in Mogadishu. One element of this success, according to the Commission, was that those who designed (through a painstaking process of negotiation) the political structures of Somaliland back in the early 1990s took the revered institution of *Tol*, Somalia's traditional courts of tribal elders, and made it into an upper chamber, a Somali House of Lords, for the new fledgling state. Thus whereas in the rest of Somalia the *Tol* was more or less abolished by the warlords and faction leaders, in Somaliland it was incorporated into the state's new institutional framework. Thus reconstituted, the *Tol*, the report believes, is an important foundation of Somaliland's political and economic success since 1993. It serves this stabilizing function because it provides a clan-based system of justice and conflict resolution which is well attuned to the needs of Somalia's social structure. The Commission thus uses this example to illustrate how important it is for those looking for solutions to the problems facing African states, including the central problem of the weakness of most African states, to pay attention to underlying cultures.

The Commission's chapter on culture identified three key areas in which, according to the Commission's consultations, many Africans believe the developed world's misunderstandings and ignorance of Africa are particularly pernicious. The first was what the Commission calls the inheritance of history, namely the clan or tribal structure of African society and the persistence of strong kinship ties into the present period. These features of modern African society have important implications for development policy, according to the Commission: 'It is not enough to dismiss patron client relations simply as channels of corruption. Development policy makers must take such culture into account in order to see how principles such as mutual accountability and responsibility can best be made to work in a modern state.'[19] Other historical factors that donors need to take into account, according to the Commission for Africa's report, include the slave trade, colonial rule and the inheritance of problematic borders and systems of land tenure, all of which in different ways had sown the seeds of future conflicts. Although the report did not spell it out, there were at least two important, if implicit, lessons in all this. First, African states had their own – often diverse – ways of doing things which needed to be factored into the design of strategies for African development. Second, several of those 'donors' now claiming to be wanting to help Africa, and none more than Britain itself, had a long and ambiguous history in Africa, including serial failures of 'development' policy, which profoundly affected the way they were perceived and treated by Africans.

The second area of common misunderstanding and ignorance on the part of outsiders, as identified in this chapter of the report, was the diversity of African peoples, states, languages and cultures. As the report put it:

> Every country has a mix of social and economic realities that differ from other countries and differ, often massively, even within one state according to divisions of ethnicity, religion, gender, generation, geography and so on ... At the very least although it may occasionally be convenient to make generalised statements about 'Africa', it is essential to pay constant regard to the continent's diversity.[20]

This was a crucial point, and one that has been often made by those familiar with African politics. But it was easier to state the problem than to suggest effective ways of dealing with it. The report of the Commission for Africa itself was guilty of making exactly the generalizations it deplored. In addressing the development conundrums of a DR Congo or a Sierra Leone, as indeed those of an Iraq or an Afghanistan, it was essential to understand the basis of local power structures, the allegiances that underpin them and the motivations of those who mediate them. But to do so called for resources, effort and long-term commitment, and a readiness to challenge and dispel the cherished assumptions of politicians back home.

The third, and perhaps the most important, misunderstanding of African culture by external policy-makers identified by the Commission is the failure to understand the significance and potential of Africa's 'invisible' social and political networks. Here the Commission's report came close to a powerful critique of the 'failed states' analysis of Africa which underpinned the rest of the report and much of UK policy towards Africa. The main thrust of the 'failed states' approach to Africa, given extra urgency by 9/11, is that 'failed states' like Afghanistan and Somalia pose serious threats not only to their own people but also to global security. They therefore need to be transformed by radical and interventionist policies making use if necessary of military as well as economic and diplomatic instruments. But, as the Commission points out, in many so-called failed states the state itself has become 'an irrelevance or a burden' for many – 'perhaps a majority' – of its citizens. 'But', the report continues, 'that does not mean that there are no effective non-state forms of governance. For many people, their primary loyalty remains with the family, clan tribe or other social networks.'[21] According to the Commission, these networks are a source of huge social and economic capital which is 'crucial' to the survival strategies of many Africans. The report does not say so explicitly, but this is not just about the survival strategies of the poor, but for the rich too. In most African states the informal economy is much larger than the formal economy. It is therefore in Africa's informal economy – defined as economic activity not included in a nation's data on gross domestic product, and not subject to formal contracts, licensing and taxation – that most actual economic development takes place. Yet in their economic development policies donors almost entirely ignore this central fact of African economic

77

life. Informal economies are largely neglected by development economists. The official statistics on which policy-makers base their decisions address only formal economic activity. Thus they are not just unreliable for the usual reasons of system failures within the formal economy. They are completely misleading. And when donors do pay attention to the informal economic networks they do so only to criminalize them, to stigmatize them as an aberration, and to use them to explain away the failures of their own policies.[22]

It was not just Africa's non-state economic networks which donors either ignored or regarded with suspicion, according to the report. They also had trouble adjusting to the expanding religious and ideological networks, both Christian and Muslim, which were thriving in an environment of state failure. The report tiptoed carefully around this sensitive issue, pointing out that 'religion can also be a vehicle for fraud, criminality, human rights abuses and extremism'. The report did point out, however, that religious networks and ideologies had grown in influence because they had been able to provide essential economic and social services which the state was no longer able or willing to provide. It could have added that one of the reasons why African states were no longer able or willing to provide such services was because they had adopted flawed development policies forced on them by the donors. Here, as elsewhere in this chapter, the Commission did not offer any solutions to the problem of the donors' cultural 'misunderstandings and ignorance', which, the report said, so often lead to the failure of development policies. This was a serious shortcoming because, as the report itself underlined, external prescriptions 'succeed only where they work with the grain of African worldviews. They fail where they ignore, or do not understand, the cultural suppositions of the people they seek to address.'[23]

The Somaliland example evoked at the outset of the report's

chapter on culture invited three pertinent criticisms of Western policy towards the rest of Somalia in the aftermath of the collapse of Somalia's central government. All three illustrated the continuing failure of Western donors to understand politics and culture. First, all regional and international interventions in Somalia had failed to learn the clear lessons of the experience of Somaliland: the need for an internal process that makes imaginative use of traditional institutions such as the *Tol* system of clan-based justice and conflict resolution and empowers those actors who have a genuine interest in peace. Instead they had promoted externally led processes that had empowered those actors who bore the greatest responsibility for Somalia's failure and were least capable of or interested in securing stability for Somalia, namely the warlords and faction and militia leaders.

Second, Somaliland's success as a model of post-conflict state reconfiguration and reconstruction also provided a direct counter-argument to the proposition put forward in the report that what weak African states needed was a massive injection of development assistance. There were good grounds for believing that one of the most important reasons why Somaliland's leaders were able, in the early and difficult days of their secession from the anarchic and conflict-ridden rump of Somalia, to avoid conflict to the extent that they did was that Somaliland, unrecognized by the rest of the world, was explicitly and deliberately excluded from benefiting from significant quantities of donor development assistance. The benefits were clear: conflicts over control of foreign aid were avoided – because the aid was not forthcoming; Somaliland was forced to fall back on developing its own commercial, agricultural and industrial resources; the Somaliland government was not burdened with the time-consuming distraction of having to manage the often contradictory policy demands of the donors; and crucially the government was accountable for its own mistakes and therefore was able to learn from them rather than blame them on the donors.

The third point about the Western approach to Somalia right up until the present was that it had signally failed to develop a realistic policy with regard to the religious dimension of political developments in the country since the early 1990s. Rather than acknowledging that political Islam, which expanded rapidly into the vacuum left by the collapse of the government, represented an opportunity for stability in Somalia, the donors, along with Somalia's neighbours, Ethiopia and Kenya, saw it only as a threat to be eliminated, if necessary by military force, whatever the consequences for the security and safety of Somalia's people or for the country's longer-term political future.

The failure of the Commission for Africa in this chapter on culture to make serious recommendations, aside from the platitudinous exhortation to work with the grain of African worldviews, was not surprising. Whatever the rhetoric, donor development policy has always been incapable of allowing developing countries to choose their own development paths suited to their own cultural, sociological and political circumstances. Indeed, where successful development has taken place it has almost always been because governments chose their own paths, often against the advice and instructions of the development diktats of the day. If taken to their logical conclusion, the arguments put forward in this part of the Commission for Africa's report would pull the rug out from under the donors' developmentalist approach to dealing with Africa. Perhaps the only sensible recommendation would have been for the UK and the other donors to go away and reconsider the assumption that their own and Africa's interests were best served by throwing more and more of their taxpayers' money at the problems of poverty and instability in Africa.

International priorities and national interests

In Africa economic development, framed in terms of poverty reduction, was the overarching objective of UK policy, mainly thanks to DfID. But UK policy towards Africa could not be separated from the rest of UK foreign policy any more than Africa itself could be separated from the rest of the world. Poverty reduction in Africa had to take its place in the queue for the government's attention and resources along with other objectives and priorities. These were quite explicitly spelled out by the FCO in a 2006 White Paper. The top seven priorities were:

> 1. Making the world safer from global terrorism and weapons of mass destruction; 2. Reducing the harm to the UK from international crime, including drug trafficking, people smuggling and money laundering; 3. Preventing and resolving conflict through a strong international system; 4. Building an effective and globally competitive EU in a secure neighbourhood; 5. Supporting the UK economy and business through an open and expanding global economy, science and innovation and secure energy supplies; 6. Achieving climate security by promoting a faster transition to a sustainable, low carbon global economy; 7. Promoting sustainable development and poverty reduction underpinned by human rights, democracy, good governance and protection of the environment; and 8. Managing migration and combating illegal immigration.[24]

British policy-makers argued that all these objectives were interrelated. In Africa, where the bulk of government money was being spent on poverty reduction, they argued that reducing poverty and stimulating economic development were the best ways of achieving many of the UK's other objectives: dealing with terrorism and crime, supporting UK business, securing energy supplies, and managing migration. In theory this made good sense. In practice these important objectives remained

The policy

key priorities in their own right which were dealt with as such without much regard to poverty reduction and economic development. In the next chapter I will examine some of the dilemmas thrown up by the pursuit of competing and sometimes contradictory objectives. But here it is necessary to outline in a little more detail how the UK pursued some of its non-developmental objectives in Africa.

Counterterrorism UK counterterrorism policy was built on four pillars: to prevent terrorism by addressing the sources of radicalization and recruitment; to prevent attacks by disrupting terrorists' plans and activities; to protect from attacks by making UK targets at home and abroad more secure; and to prepare for attacks by building the capacity to respond to them quickly. In Africa a UK terrorism prevention policy was slow to get off the ground because DfID, which was best placed to address the sources of radicalization and recruitment, was not willing to be diverted from its poverty reduction mission. The protection element of the policy was limited to making embassies more secure and issuing travel advisories to British citizens in areas where there was a perceived threat and strict travel guidelines to British officials. The main focus of the counterterrorism strategy as it developed in Africa was therefore the effort to disrupt terrorist activities and capacities and to build the capacity of friendly African states to help in that effort. Here the UK, with the United States in the lead, extended what it was doing in South Asia and the Middle East to Africa on the grounds that large parts of the continent were a potential theatre for terrorist activities. The rationale was based on hard evidence that Islamist extremists were operating in Africa. Al-Qaeda had carried out terrorist attacks on Western targets in Kenya and Tanzania in 1998 and they struck again at Israeli targets in Kenya in 2002. The fear was that, unless checked, terrorist groups would continue to exploit

Africa's weak and failing states and its 'ungoverned spaces' to extend their influence and reach.

Consequently Washington and London stepped up their counterterrorism operations in those parts of Africa that were seen as most vulnerable to terrorist infiltration: the Red Sea coast, Somalia, Sudan, the Sahara, etc. For example, the Pentagon set up the Combined Joint Task Force in Djibouti to monitor the Red Sea and the Horn of Africa for terrorist activity and launched a series of counterterrorism and intelligence-gathering coopera- tion programmes with several African governments across the continent. The UK was discreetly involved in these operations. The new counterterrorism dimension to US and UK policy in Africa inevitably led to a distinct, if sometimes secret, change in the relationship between Washington and London on the one hand and a number of African governments on the other, including those of all North African states, Sudan, Ethiopia, Kenya, and most of the countries of the Sahelian region on the southern fringes of the Sahara. Already in the 1990s there had been a significant militarization of the American, European and United Nations approach to Africa because of concerns over the spread of internal and regional conflicts. This trend towards militarization was now accelerated after 2001 in the name of counterterrorism. In 2006 it led to the creation for the first time of a separate US military command with responsibility for over- seeing US defence policy in Africa, AFRICOM. Significantly this was the same year which saw the Americans launch their first major counterterrorism operation in Africa. Concerned by the growing influence of Somalia's Islamic Courts Union (ICU), with alleged links to al-Qaeda, the CIA and the Pentagon launched a campaign against the ICU using the Ethiopian army and allied Somali factions as proxy forces. By the end of the year this had led to a full-scale Ethiopian invasion and occupation of Mogadishu, apparently with full diplomatic and political cover from the UN

and the EU, with the UK pushing its sometimes reluctant EU
partners towards the hard-line US position.

Energy security and commercial interests In the first ten years
of Labour government fears about dwindling oil reserves increased significantly. These fears were stoked by massive economic and industrial growth in Asia and acute instability in
key oil-producing regions. As a consequence there was a frantic
search for new and secure energy supplies on the part of all the
industrialized nations, including China. Several African countries
such as Angola and Nigeria were already important oil producers
and new fields had been identified in the Gulf of Guinea. There
was also untapped oil in East Africa, especially in Sudan, which,
with China's help, started producing oil in 1999, transforming
the complex and violent politics of that country. As the report
of the Commission for Africa noted, sub-Saharan Africa held 7
per cent of the world's oil reserves, and it was predicted that
by 2015 the United States would source 25 per cent of its oil
imports from West Africa.[25] The UK also has a significant stake
in the security of world oil supplies. According to the FCO, 'as
the UK relies increasingly on imported energy, we need to work
internationally to support open and diversified energy markets
that ensure long-term security of supply'.[26]

Furthermore, as noted in Chapter 1, UK firms had an important commercial stake in energy production and other sectors in
several parts of the continent. BP was one of the leading investors
in Angola's oil industry and the Anglo-Dutch Shell oil company
was the leading and longest-operating oil company in Nigeria's
troubled Niger Delta. Several British mining companies such as
Rio Tinto, Anglo-American, Lonrho and Ashanti Gold had investments in African countries. British military companies such as
BAE were active in selling arms to Africa, with strong support
from the British government. Private security companies, a field

in which British firms were important players, found in Africa's conflict zones and insecurity an ideal and lucrative environment in which to expand their business. As the FCO's White Paper on international priorities put it, 'trade and investment are essential elements of UK prosperity and contribute to UK productivity. Working through UK Trade and Investment ... we will help the UK economy to respond to the challenges of globalization by supporting UK companies in developing their business internationally.'[27]

Migration Africa's political and economic crises of the 1990s, combined with accelerating globalization, had added considerably to the trend of African immigration to Europe, with many now arriving in the UK as asylum seekers and as clandestine immigrants from Africa's hot spots. According to the Foreign Office, visa applications to the UK more than doubled from 1.5 million per year in 1999/2000 to over 3 million in 2007/08. Home Office figures for asylum applications (which by no means cover the whole gamut of immigration) reveal a strong link between conflict and immigration to the UK. In the eight years from 1997 Somalia has consistently provided the largest numbers of asylum seekers in the UK, peaking at 7,495 in 1997. Large numbers of asylum seekers have also fled to the UK from wars and repression in DR Congo (2,215 in 2002), Zimbabwe (7,655 in 2002), Sierra Leone (1,940 in 2001), Sudan (1,305 in 2004), Angola (1,420 in 2002) and Eritrea (1,760 in 2005).[28] African immigration to the UK obviously had serious political implications. Commentary and reporting on immigration issues in the British media took up much more space than reporting of the crises from which immigrants were fleeing. Polls and the media reflected increasing concern about the economic and cultural impact of non-European immigration and about perceived failures of 'multiculturalism' and integration. After 9/11, and even more after the July 2005 bombings

85

in London, an important security dimension to the problem of immigration emerged as it became apparent that recent and not-so-recent immigrants, including some of African descent, were involved in terrorist plots against the British public.

When it came to immigration there was potentially a close alignment between the interests of the UK and other EU members and those of African states. If African states were stabilized, conflicts were resolved and economic development were achieved, then Africans would have less motivation to seek refuge or a better life in Europe. The immigration crisis in Europe, however, could not wait for the stabilization of Africa. EU countries, including the UK, were already closing their frontiers to migration and imposing ever stricter visa regulations. This was adding not only to the desperation and misery of those seeking an exit route from African crises but also to the difficulties of African states and UN agencies trying to manage the flows of migrants and refugees. Furthermore, while they understandably wanted to control their borders, some EU states with ageing and falling indigenous populations welcomed the immigration of certain categories of skilled workers and professionals. This contributed to a brain drain from African countries that needed exactly these people to help them rebuild economies devastated by war and instability. The phenomenon was only partially compensated for by the large financial remittances that expatriates sent back to family members in Africa.

Climate change The UK was one of the leading Western nations to start sounding the alarm about climate change from 2003 onwards. The UK government made climate change a theme of its chairmanship of the G8 in 2005, and Margaret Beckett, a former environment minister who replaced Jack Straw as Foreign Secretary in May 2006, pushed it high up the UK's foreign policy agenda during her year in office. The main objective of the UK's policy was to get international agreement on reducing emissions of carbon dioxide, which most scientists agreed was responsible for global warming. But the UK was slow to integrate its policy on climate change with its development policies in Africa and other poor parts of the world. Africa contributed very little to the carbon emissions that were thought to be responsible for global warming. But at the same time Africa was among the most vulnerable to the effects of climate change, as recent events had shown. The 1997/98 El Niño in southern Africa caused widespread famine and resulted in billions of dollars' worth of agricultural losses. In 2000 tropical cyclones caused floods in Mozambique that reduced the annual growth rate from 8 to 2 per cent. In the same year the World Bank had to step in with a $72 million emergency loan for Kenya when drought in East Africa reduced Kenya's hydroelectric power capacity. Droughts across the Sahelian region contributed to famines in Niger, Mali and Chad in 2005 and 2006. The following year, 2007, the region experienced the worst flooding in living memory. Some even linked the conflicts in Darfur and Somalia to climate change. Rising sea levels threatened coastal areas, including many of Africa's largest cities. Because of lack of investment, poverty and poor governance, Africa's adaptive capacity to meet the challenges posed by climate change was far lower than that of rich countries. As the FCO acknowledged, 'climate change will increasingly be a barrier to development and a factor in instability, natural disasters, migration and perhaps conflict. The long-term impact could be particularly severe in vulnerable areas of Africa.'[29]

Climate change raised important and difficult new questions about the UK's policy in Africa. Was there such a thing as climate-friendly economic development? If there was, could Africa afford it, and was the UK promoting it in Africa? Were rich nations that had contributed most to climate change morally obliged to compensate African nations that were most vulnerable to its

87

effects? Should the donors refocus their efforts in Africa towards building the capacity of African states and societies to adapt to climate change? Were the donors any more capable of achieving that objective than they were capable of reducing poverty in Africa? Would the donors be able to address poverty and climate change in Africa at the same time? How far would the impact of climate change on developed nations' economies and societies affect aid flows to Africa? Was climate change going to be the new scapegoat for the continuing failure of the donors' development policies in Africa?

Networking and jet-setting

The ambitious programme of interventionist transformation that Britain developed under Tony Blair was not something that the UK would be able to implement alone. It depended on the cooperation of the African leaders whom Blair had courted in the run-up to the G8 summit of 2005. And it also depended on the cooperation of Britain's international allies, the United States, Canada, Japan and above all its fellow members of the European Union, especially France and Germany. Blair sought to bring these allies around to his programme for Africa, and he met with some success at the Gleneagles summit and elsewhere in securing agreements on increased aid and debt relief. There were, however, limits to how far the Americans and Europeans were prepared to go, especially on reducing trade barriers. It was felt by many that the 'enhanced partnership' idea that was supposed to be embodied by NEPAD had not worked out as planned. The Africans were not fulfilling their side of the bargain. And until they did more aid, debt relief, investment and concessions on trade were not warranted. That is why Blair felt he needed the support of another set of actors: celebrities who could mobilize public opinion around the world in support of his plans for massively increasing assistance to Africa. This was the rationale behind Blair's efforts to get Bob Geldof and Bono involved in promoting his policy, the Live Eight concerts, the Make Poverty History campaign and all the rest of it. With Blair at the helm, Britain's Africa policy could not just be a policy. It had to be an international event played out in the glare of the global media. Paradoxically the divisions, resentments and suspicions within the EU and between the EU and the United States created by the invasion of Iraq did not significantly undermine Blair's efforts to achieve a consensus on Africa among these allies. At a time of deep crisis in the transatlantic alliance over Iraq, both the pro-Iraq and the anti-Iraq camps were keen to find areas of common interest, and Africa was one of them. Much more challenging, however, was the emergence on the African scene over the first ten years of Labour government of a new and powerful external player: China.

The European Union The EU was the biggest provider of development assistance to Africa and its biggest economic and trade partner. It was therefore a potentially influential player. Its relationship with Africa was formalized by the Cotonou agreement of 2000, the successor to the Lomé agreement between the EU and African, Pacific and Caribbean states, as well as by a series of partnership agreements between the EU and individual African countries and subregional organizations. EU policy towards Africa was broadly consistent with that of the UK. This was not surprising as the UK, together with France, had long played an influential role in determining the EU's approach. From 1997 to 2003 the UK provided between 25 and 31 per cent of its total overseas development aid expenditure through the EU.[30] Inevitably, however, in an organization of fifteen member states in 1997 rising to twenty-seven by 2007, the EU–African relationship had its weaknesses. EU positions and policies had to be negotiated among all member states, and this took time and effort and usually ended up with the EU taking the position of the lowest common denominator. In spite of efforts to strengthen the EU's external relations decision-making machinery through the Common Foreign and Security Policy and other institutional reforms in Brussels, the policies that emerged were often bland, predictable and incoherent. The weaknesses and inconsistencies of decision-making in Brussels thus reduced both the effectiveness of EU aid and the EU's political leverage in African politics.

Leverage was also undermined by frequent disagreements within the EU between the two major European players in Africa – France and the UK – with each seeking to protect its own sphere of influence. Where other EU members had historic interests – Italy in the Horn of Africa and Portugal in its former southern African colonies – these states also sought to protect their parochial interests. These intra-EU rivalries sometimes allowed African states to play EU donors off against one another. In 1998 Robin Cook sought to resolve some of London's differences with Paris on Africa through the so-called St Malo process, which led to more frequent bilateral meetings on Africa. Relations between the French and British at the level of foreign ministry officials were reasonably cooperative and led to a number of good initiatives, for example on building African peacekeeping capacity. But there was less openness between Number 10 and the French presidency (which had traditionally managed the most important aspects of France's Africa policy). Relations between Blair and President Jacques Chirac were exacerbated by the sharp disagreements over Iraq, even if this did not really affect Franco-British cooperation on Africa. An EU stumbling block for the UK's ambitions for Africa, however, was the EU's highly protectionist Common Agricultural Policy, which was seen by the Commission for Africa, along with other protectionist policies of the industrialized countries, as a major hindrance to the ability of African producers to compete on a level playing field.

The United States Under President Bill Clinton, US policy towards Africa had moved from a period of reduced engagement after the Somalia débâcle in 1994 to increased engagement in the later years of the administration. This was stimulated both by guilt over its failure to stop the 1994 genocide in Rwanda and by the growing realization of Africa's energy potential. Fears that a new Republican administration would reduce its assistance to and engagement with Africa after President George Bush's 2000 election proved unfounded. Bush's engagement with Africa was founded on a mixture of influences. First, there was the new focus on counterterrorism in Africa in the aftermath of 9/11. Second, the Christian right, an important element of Bush's electoral power base, was very active in Africa (and especially active in relation to Sudan). Third, there had been strong criticism (including from his own party) of Clinton's failure to prevent the 1994 genocide in Rwanda. 'Not on my watch,' Bush is reported to have jotted down on a memo prepared for him summarizing criticisms of Clinton's failure.[31] Finally, oil interests in Africa inevitably loomed even larger under the leadership of former oil executives Bush and Vice-President Dick Cheney than they had under Clinton.

The UK was broadly aligned with the USA on the important aspects of its policy in Africa, and the two sides cooperated and shared information on a daily basis in Washington, London and in African capitals. In particular the UK and the United States worked closely together on securing the north–south peace deal in Sudan, on the crisis in Darfur, on building Africa's peacekeeping capacity and on counterterrorism. Inevitably there was commercial competition, especially in the energy sector, but this was not allowed to sour cooperation in other areas. On economic development, however, DfID was wary of the conservative approach of the Bush administration. Clare Short was deeply distrustful of the Republicans in general. This mirrored her increasing discontent with the direction of Blair's partnership with Bush in counterterrorism after 9/11 and led to her resignation over the Iraq war. Short also felt that Bush was not fully committed to poverty reduction, at least not to her own conception of how it was to be achieved. In fact US aid to Africa increased considerably under Bush, who also signed the Africa Growth and Opportunity Act which granted privileged trading access to US markets for chosen African allies. But US aid remained far from the OECD target of 0.7 per cent of gross national income. British development officials were also irritated by the influence of the Christian right on US aid policy, in particular the policy on combating HIV with its insistence, against all the evidence, that encouragement of sexual abstinence was the key to solving the HIV crisis. On trade too the UK was disappointed by the United States' protectionist positions at the World Trade Organization negotiations, in particular its reluctance to reduce subsidies to its cotton farmers. DfID felt these damaged African economic prospects. But Washington reasonably enough pointed out that as long as the EU's Common Agricultural Policy remained in place the UK was hardly in a position to lecture the United States on trade.

China Like other Western donors, the UK was slow off the mark in recognizing the importance of China's growing engagement in Africa in the 1990s. It was only after the start of the new millennium that the true significance of China's increasing trade, investments, loans and development assistance in Africa began to sink in. Even so, the Commission for Africa's report hardly mentioned the significance of China's new role in Africa. In 2006 trade between China and Africa was worth over £30 billion, an increase of 40 per cent over the previous year. This made China Africa's third-largest trading partner after the EU and the United States. In the first nine months of 2006, China committed almost

£7 billion to investment in infrastructure in Africa, more than all the OECD countries combined. In November 2006, forty-eight African heads of state attended a China–Africa summit in Beijing at which China announced it would double its aid to Africa by 2009 and expand access for African products to China's market. China's growing involvement in Africa presented both risks and opportunities. The main risk was that because China was historically reluctant to interfere in 'sovereign affairs' and was not noted for its commitment to democracy and human rights at home, its economic assistance to Africa would be free of the sorts of political conditions set by Western donors and would therefore undermine the 'good governance agenda' by which the Europeans and the Americans appeared to set so much store. In effect, this argument went, China's strings-free aid and investment undermined the West's leverage to bring about the kind of political reform it saw as necessary to kick-start developmental states. On the other hand there were opportunities for Africa in China's engagement. First, China produced a wide range of goods that African consumers wanted to buy at prices they could afford. Second, China's hunger for energy and raw materials was a welcome boost to the prices of African commodities after a long period of relative stagnation. Third, China's presence in Africa's development and investment markets meant that the West would have to improve the services it was offering if it was to remain competitive.

Much of the European and American concern over China focused on China's relationship with those countries that were most seriously at odds with Washington and London, principally Zimbabwe and Sudan. China, it was noted, supplied arms to both countries and in Sudan it was the main foreign customer for and investor in the new oil industry, revenues from which were used to prop up the manipulative Khartoum regime and bankroll its brutal suppression of the rebellion in Darfur. These concerns were justified. But there were double standards at work here. It was not so long since the West had adopted policies towards Africa which were even more destabilizing than China's. Even now, for reasons of strategic self-interest, the United States and Europe were supplying aid and military assistance to governments like those of Ethiopia and Nigeria, which were engaged in the violent suppression of unrest. Belatedly the UK recognized that China had become a key player in Africa and that managing the risks and opportunities of China's role would require a lot of hard work across the whole range of issues – managing conflicts, improving governance, reducing poverty, aid, debt and trade. Here again was a body of work for which the diplomatic, linguistic and analytical skills of the FCO would be necessary as well as DfID's developmental expertise.

International institutions From the beginning of the Labour government in 1997, the UK was particularly active at the UN and elsewhere in pursuing its goal of 'preventing and resolving conflict through a strong international system'. It was not just a question of the UK taking a lead in cajoling the UN to take a more activist, interventionist and effective approach to emerging crises, whether in Sierra Leone, Liberia, DR Congo, Burundi or Kosovo. The UK was also actively involved in efforts to strengthen the capacity of the international and regional institutions to prevent, manage and resolve conflicts, to build peace in the aftermath of conflicts and to protect civilians from crimes against humanity and war crimes. This was an area where the UK made a positive contribution, albeit one that was badly tarnished by its involvement in Iraq.

Labour quite quickly understood that effective conflict management required an approach that addressed the whole continuum of conflict, from prevention and containment of conflicts, to peacekeeping and mediation, to post-conflict reconstruction and peace-building. In all these phases of conflict management it would be necessary to work simultaneously on several fronts: diplomatic, political, military, economic, judicial, social, educational, etc. Furthermore it was not enough to work only at the national level. On the one hand it was necessary to go down to the grassroots to address local problems, dealing with the non-state as well as the state actors. On the other it was also necessary to tackle the broader regional and international dimensions and linkages of state failure and conflict. This was a very considerable agenda, and in order to put itself in a better position to start to address it, the UK government set up two 'conflict prevention pools', one for Africa and another for the rest of the world, which encouraged the MoD, the FCO and DfID to work together on conflict management and made available funds (about £50 million in each pool) that could be quickly accessed to deal with emerging crises. Mechanisms were later established to enable the Home Office to contribute policing expertise and personnel to peacekeeping and to enable the Department of Trade and Industry to get involved in anti-corruption work in the post-conflict phase.

The UK also sought to strengthen the ability and capacity of international and regional organizations such as the UN, the World Bank, the EU, NATO and, in Africa, the African Union and subregional bodies to manage conflicts. After the publication of the highly critical report of Lakhdar Brahimi and his panel on UN peace operations in 2000, the UK used its clout in New York to push for reform of UN peacekeeping along the lines recommended by the report, i.e. in critical areas of doctrine, capacity, competence, resources, strategic planning, management and the rapid deployment capability of UN peacekeeping operations. Equally the UK, along with France and the United States, was active in building the capacity of African military forces to participate in UN and AU peacekeeping operations, as well as providing them directly with the logistical assistance they needed to deploy and supply their peacekeepers. The idea of creating five African subregional stand-by peacekeeping forces for deployment in African conflicts was a British one pushed through in the G8's 'action plan' for Africa in 2003. The British also provided the funds and the initiative (and the senior military staff) to establish the Kofi Annan International Peacekeeping Training Centre in Ghana. The UK estimates that, by 2010, it will have trained 17,000 peacekeeping troops as part of its peacekeeping training programme, either directly through British teams based in South Africa and Kenya or indirectly through organizations supported by the UK. These efforts may well have contributed to the improvements that took place in UN peacekeeping between 1997 and 2007.

Another important contribution of the UK was in the area of international justice. Here the UK was again among those states at the forefront of efforts in seeking to harness the evolving mechanisms of international justice, such as the International Criminal Court (ICC), to international efforts to protect civilians from war crimes and crimes against humanity. When it took power in 1997 the Labour government reversed the policy of the outgoing Conservative government and supported international negotiations that led to the creation of the ICC (whose first investigations were all in Africa – in DR Congo, Uganda, Sudan and the Central African Republic). After the Republicans came to power in the United States in 2001, the Labour government even managed to dilute the Bush administration's strenuous efforts to obstruct the work of the ICC. It did this by demonstrating to Washington the ICC's value in putting pressure on the Sudanese regime over Darfur. In West Africa the UK was the prime mover behind the establishment and funding of the Special Court for Sierra Leone to bring prosecutions against those responsible for war crimes in the Sierra Leone civil war, including the deposed president of Liberia, Charles Taylor. Neither the ICC nor the ad hoc tribunals in Sierra Leone and Rwanda were without their shortcomings, and they have sparked a vigorous debate about the extent to which the pursuit of international justice may actually be holding up the conclusion of peace – for example, in northern Uganda. But the UK argued with conviction that justice for the most serious war crimes and crimes against humanity was a necessary component of sustainable peace and reconciliation.

Celebrity humanitarianism Blair's populist approach to leadership and his understanding of the political power of celebrity became apparent with his virtuoso performance in reaction to the dramatic death of Diana, Princess of Wales, in August 1997. In the mid-1990s Diana had infuriated the Conservative Party by putting the weight of her international celebrity behind the NGO-led campaign for a treaty banning landmines. Conservative efforts to undermine her had backfired, leaving the government looking petty and out of touch with popular sentiment. One of the Blair government's first moves was to support the push for a treaty banning landmines.

Later, as Blair became more interested in Africa, he sought to harness the phenomenon of celebrity in support of his developmentalist agenda for the continent. This strategy had some very real advantages. Celebrity campaigners such as Bob Geldof, Bono and George Clooney had massive popular reach and were able to raise international awareness both of generic issues such as poverty and of more specific humanitarian crises such as Darfur. As Mark Malloch-Brown, now a minister for Africa in the UK government, said of the impact of the advocacy work of Hollywood stars on China's attitude to Darfur, 'Tinseltown proved momentarily better at the foreign policy game than London or Washington.'[32] Blair assiduously courted celebrities who were willing to put their names to his efforts to address poverty in

Africa and used them as a means of mobilizing international popular opinion. One effect of this was to ramp up the pressure on the other donors to sign up to Blair's proposals for a large increase in donor funding for poverty reduction efforts in Africa. Mainstream NGOs and the media encouraged celebrity humanitarianism because they too could benefit from it: the NGOs because it raised popular awareness of 'their' issues and thus stimulated the private and public charity on which they depended; the media because it made for TV good ratings and newspaper sales.

But inevitably there was also a downside to this stellar approach to humanitarianism. It tended to feed into the fairy-tale media image of Africa as a desperate continent that was unable to deal with its own problems and required the help of non-African heroes – the aid worker, the celebrity film star, the rock singer – often in the face of obstruction from African villains – warlords, corrupt rulers, ruthless militiamen, etc. This was an image that sustained the notion that Africa's problems were best solved by external interventions of one kind or another, and that Africans were either villains or helpless victims. Because the mass media on which it thrived need simple, one-dimensional messages, celebrity humanitarianism tended to simplify the issues it latched on to. On some issues this hardly mattered. The landmine campaign used simple messages. But in truth both the problem and the solution were quite straightforward. Only those who profited from the use and sale of landmines pretended otherwise. But poverty in Africa and conflict in Darfur were quite different kinds of phenomenon: in both cases the problems were multidimensional and complex and no one who had studied them seriously believed that there were any easy or obvious solutions. Distilling the issue of poverty in Africa down to the simple message that a doubling of aid and the cancellation of debt would solve it was misleading and potentially counterproductive, both because it ignored many other issues that needed to be addressed (such as conflict and governance) but also because it highlighted a course of action that was not guaranteed to produce the advertised results. Furthermore, while the use by politicians of celebrity humanitarianism may have served the useful purpose of co-opting the NGOs and the media, for that very reason it also marginalized and blunted expert criticism of the policies advocated by those same politicians.

The policy

3 | Limits of leverage

'Wealthy nations and Africa both face a choice: us, as to how far
we help Africa to take the right path; Africa as to which path to
take ... Our challenge is to support the good; Africa's challenge
is to eliminate the bad.' Tony Blair, speech in South Africa, May
2007

In the last weeks of his premiership in May 2007 Tony Blair
embarked on a valedictory tour of Africa which took him to Libya,
where he focused attention on his government's role in persuading Colonel Mu'ammer Gaddafi to give up his nuclear weapons
programme; to Sierra Leone, where he celebrated the UK's part
in resolving that country's civil war; and to South Africa, where
he had a final photo opportunity with Africa's most popular and
famous modern leader, Nelson Mandela. Significantly none of the
biggest recipients of UK aid was on Blair's itinerary. He avoided
Sudan, where, in spite of the success of the north–south peace
deal, the UK and its international partners had been unable
to stem the humanitarian catastrophe unleashed by the brutal
policies of the Khartoum government in Darfur. And he avoided
Uganda, Rwanda and Ethiopia, where limited progress on economic development and poverty reduction was badly tarnished by
serious shortcomings on human rights and political governance.
More surprisingly he did not even go to Ghana or Tanzania, where
DfID insisted its aid was making some difference – but where
poverty remained stubbornly entrenched.

Blair may well have been disappointed that there was not more
to show for his efforts in Africa in the decade from 1997. But in
itself the UK's determination to devote more time, money and

attention to addressing Africa's problems had been impressive, as was its success in convincing other important international players that Africa was worth helping. The UK could take some of the credit for the significant progress that was made in resolving and managing African conflicts from 2000 onwards and in building Africa's capacity to cooperate with the international system in that task. The UK's role in Sierra Leone stands out in particular. Furthermore, it was always clear that bringing stability and economic development to Africa was going to take time and patience as well as hard work and resources. Measured against British efforts in the Middle East, where by 2007 British policy had contributed to a very serious deterioration of stability, the UK's influence in Africa had been relatively benign.

Nevertheless, by the time Blair handed over the premiership to Gordon Brown in June 2007, implementation of the UK's African policy was already revealing some important limitations. First, experience across the continent was demonstrating that rebuilding weak and collapsed states, especially in the aftermath of armed conflict, was very difficult indeed, and there was little evidence that the remedies on offer from the UK and other donors were working. The UK's efforts had helped to push a number of failing and collapsed states back to the point at which they could have a fair shot at political and economic regeneration. And the UK had achieved this in part by fine-tuning some of the political, diplomatic, military and economic instruments of leverage. This had incidentally brought benefits for the whole world, not just Africa – for example, progress in building the institutions of international criminal justice. But nowhere had the UK's and other donors' mix of policies and interventions proved sufficient to transform a weak or failed state into a developmental state that was in a position to provide long-term security and prosperity to its citizens without open-ended external support.

Second, the UK government wielded rather less leverage and

influence over African state and non-state actors than UK politicians and officials appeared to assume. The tools of leverage, military, economic and diplomatic, were blunt, unwieldy and often ineffective means of getting both foes and allies in Africa to do what the UK thought necessary to achieve 'development'. Furthermore, what leverage there was could often be undermined by lack of coordination or outright competition between different external actors and by the contradictions within UK policy between the high-profile development and poverty reduction agenda and the more discreet determination to pursue strategic and commercial national interests, such as energy security, counterterrorism and business for UK companies.

Third, the sheer expansiveness of Blair's mission in Africa raised expectations both in London and in Africa that were almost inevitably going to be disappointed. The UK couldn't be everywhere in Africa all the time. In a vast and diverse continent of myriad challenges the government had to prioritize where and how it was going to spend its money. Therefore it had to depend on the sometimes unforthcoming cooperation of African and international partners, bilateral and multilateral, to make up the important gaps. Although Whitehall drew up elaborate frameworks, strategies and action plans, complete with performance targets, benchmarks for progress and criteria for evaluation, the actual decision-making and performance on the ground were often wanting, and the results achieved limited. This was of course completely inevitable. The problem was as much with the grand ambition of the policy itself as with implementation.

Even in the most favourable of circumstances, the objectives set by the UK government in Africa from about 2000 onwards were astonishingly comprehensive. But after 2001 the international context in which Blair would have to implement his Africa programme was far from ideal. Afghanistan and then Iraq would come to eat up massive military, diplomatic and economic resources. They would divert the political attention of all the three departments of state that were charged with implementing the programme, and of the prime minister himself. They would put pressure on government finances and on the capacity of the armed forces to deploy in Africa. And they would damage the international reputation of the UK around the world, especially among Muslims. Given this background, the wide scope of the UK's objective, the limited leverage available to achieve its goals, and the lack of solid backing from other key international actors, it is not surprising that there were some who wondered whether Blair's Africa policy was intended more to impress upon the world – and on British voters – the prime minister's good intentions, and perhaps to compensate for the failures in Iraq, than to be taken seriously as a viable and realistic programme of action.

Making a difference?

As already noted, DfID became the motor that drove UK policy in Africa from 1997 onwards for the simple reason that it was spending serious money in Africa. As the cost of DfID's bilateral country and regional programmes in sub-Saharan Africa increased sharply from about £300 million in 1997/98 to £1.25 billion in 2006/07, DfID's influence over the decision-making process inevitably grew.[1] DfID was obliged by its mandate from the Treasury and by the 2002 International Development Act to spend its budget in a manner 'likely to contribute to poverty reduction'. Africa was an obvious candidate for such spending, and by 2005/06 DfID's budget for Africa had risen to almost 55 per cent of its total bilateral assistance for the whole world. But there were many poor African countries to choose from. By 2005 almost 90 per cent of DfID's programme allocation for Africa was going to sixteen priority countries identified in the department's public service agreement with the Treasury (which set out spending targets and performance benchmarks). These countries were Ghana, Nigeria, Sierra Leone, Sudan, Ethiopia, DR Congo, Rwanda, Uganda, Kenya, Tanzania, Zambia, Malawi, Mozambique, Zimbabwe, Lesotho and South Africa (see table below). Most of these were former colonies of the UK. They were consequently also countries with which the UK had long-standing business ties. It was not surprising perhaps that all the UK's major trading partners in Africa were listed as priority countries by DfID.

The four countries that were not former British colonies were DR Congo, Rwanda, Ethiopia and Mozambique. Of those only Mozambique was a significant recipient of UK bilateral aid prior to 1997. Because of its proximity to South Africa, Mozambique, unlike the other three, was also a country where the UK had developed significant business interests. Ethiopia and Rwanda were chosen for special treatment by DfID in part for personal reasons: Clare Short was impressed by what she saw as the commitment of both Meles Zenawi and Paul Kagame to economic development. The UK was drawn into paying more attention to DR Congo both because of the seriousness of the conflicts there and because those conflicts were inextricably linked with the political interests of Rwanda and Uganda, the UK's two main clients in the region. Ethiopia was a priority for the UK after 9/11 for strategic reasons, though tensions emerged between DfID and the FCO over the relative importance that London should attach to strategic and developmental concerns, with DfID officials fearing that the focus on counterterrorism would undermine its development objectives.

DfID's priorities within each country reflected the mix of reasons why the department chose to focus on that particular country. In relatively stable countries the sectors that received the most funding were economic infrastructure, health, education and governance. Over the first seven or eight years of Labour govern-

TABLE 3.1 DfID programme allocations in priority countries in sub-Saharan Africa (£1,000)

	1997/98	1999/2000	2001/02	2005/06
Ghana	15,087	42,624	51,615	85,387
Nigeria	6,984	13,342	19,725	80,952
Sierra Leone	2,943	29,649	34,408	32,093
Sudan	n/a	3,232	5,286	130,835
Ethiopia	3,415	6,372	11,390	62,018
DR Congo	n/a	1,322	5,558	51,892
Rwanda	0	14,240	26,891	68,128
Uganda	45,417	51,988	66,665	67,337
Kenya	25,675	24,232	24,925	64,219
Tanzania	39,987	61,976	63,254	109,199
Zambia	12,127	10,522	39,113	47,128
Malawi	24,235	45,725	42,058	70,014
Mozambique	19,452	20,980	38,567	56,237
Zimbabwe	10,771	11,638	14,699	37,336
South Africa	22,944	29,570	n/a	35,343
Lesotho	4,175	2,490	n/a	n/a
AFRICA TOTAL	297,250	402,351	532,497	1,097,184

ment the balance shifted away from the economic sector towards the social sectors and governance. After 2005 there was a slight move back towards the economic sector in line with shifting development fashion and the needs of states for reconstruction in the aftermath of conflicts. Increasingly, where DfID believed there existed a real commitment to poverty reduction and economic development on the part of the recipient government, the department was keen to provide aid in the form of direct transfers of money known as 'direct budget support'. By 2004/05 DfID was providing direct budget support to seventeen African countries (including several which were not priority countries). The thinking behind the move towards direct transfers of money was that, where governments showed genuine commitment and

Limits of leverage

had put in place donor-approved poverty reduction strategies and proper accounting mechanisms, aid provided in this form was much more efficient and effective. It cut out the need for DfID to manage development projects itself or to subcontract them to international NGOs. But more importantly it gave the recipient of aid control and 'ownership' of its development strategy. A potential problem with this type of aid, however, was that it greatly empowered those who controlled public funds in the recipient state. It was also much more difficult to account for how it was spent.

In countries in conflict and crisis such as Sudan, Zimbabwe and DR Congo, where direct budget support was out of the question, a large part of DfID's spend was on humanitarian assistance. But DfID, as well as the FCO and the MoD, also struggled with the problem of how to deal with fragile states that were coming out of or at risk of going into violent conflict. How was one to nurture in the very adverse circumstances of violent conflict, or post-conflict instability, the creation of states capable of providing security to their people and of managing their own economic and political development? One mechanism for addressing this problem was the UK government's Africa conflict prevention pool, established in 2001 and jointly managed by DfID, the MoD and the FCO. This exercise in 'joined up government' sought to pool the expertise and resources of the different departments engaged in managing and preventing conflict. But in the first few years of the pool's existence about half of its annual budget of £50 million was spent on Sierra Leone (mostly on retraining the army and police), leaving very little money in the conflict pool to deal with more deadly African conflicts such as in DR Congo, or in parts of the continent that were of greater strategic concern to the UK, such as Sudan and Somalia. The dilemmas of dealing with difficult states are explored in more detail in the next section.

The increasing focus of external development actors on weak

states, governance and security from the mid-1990s onwards has to some extent obscured the arguments about macroeconomic policy which dominated the development debate in the 1980s and early 1990s. But those arguments have not gone away. Critics of the so-called 'Washington consensus' charge that the UK and its donor allies are still seeking to use aid conditionality to ram privatization and economic liberalization down the throats of African governments. A more subtle critique is that while liberalization may be a good end in itself, development ideology and practice have given free markets a bad name by arrogantly imposing liberalization in a wholly ineffective and damaging way. Thus the structural adjustment failures of the 1990s and their disastrous political and economic consequences can partially explain the populist success of the neo-socialist backlash in Latin America, Vladimir Putin's crackdown on democracy and civil society in Russia and Mugabe's attacks on political dissent in Zimbabwe. Development failures of the World Bank and the IMF may also help to explain the rise of Islamic fundamentalism in the Middle East, where '$154 billion in foreign aid between 1980 and 2001, 45 structural adjustment loans and "expert" advice produced zero per capita GDP growth'.[2]

The rhetoric has changed, of course, since the days of structural adjustment. The new development-speak coming out of donor capitals talks of the importance of 'local ownership' of development strategies, 'mutual accountability' between aid donors and recipients, and 'balanced partnerships'.[3] But though the language may be more politically correct (and less comprehensible), DfID's development bureaucrats are no less prescriptive and doctrinaire. Woe betide the African government that does not sign up to the shibboleths of 'pro-poor economic growth', 'good governance' and 'stable investment climates'. And even if DfID sometimes appears to distance itself from the stricter development frameworks of the World Bank, the IMF and the

European Commission, it would not make much difference, as 40 per cent of the UK's development assistance is provided through multilateral agencies.

Another criticism of DfID's development efforts is that they defy accurate or convincing evaluation. At a macro level it is extremely difficult to identify what the impacts of development (or conflict management) programmes really are, and whether they achieve their stated objectives. This raises extremely worrying questions about DfID's accountability. In often complex and difficult political and economic environments it is very hard to prove that x development policy or programme has resulted in or contributed to y good outcome, or indeed to z bad outcome. Unless the government can show convincingly that the more than £1 billion DfID now spends in Africa has a positive impact (whether in terms of poverty reduction or in terms of making the UK more secure), UK taxpayers are unlikely to support its work ad infinitum. So far DfID has been shielded from serious accountability by the fact that, according to opinion polls, the British public genuinely cares about the objective of reducing poverty in places like Africa and does not know very much about the role of UK and multilateral development bureaucracies in achieving that objective. The media hype about poverty reduction generated by Live Eight, Comic Relief and celebrity campaigners – hype that has been consistently encouraged by the UK government – further muddies the waters of popular perceptions and masks the tough questions that need asking. Measured by DfID's own performance targets, Whitehall's development work in Africa has not been very successful. For example, Target 1 of DfID's public service agreement with the Treasury is progress towards achieving the sixteen Millennium Development Goals in DfID's priority countries in Africa. In its 2007 annual report DfID acknowledged that there was no progress or negative progress towards achieving ten of the goals and insufficient progress towards achieving six of them. Of course, there have been some success stories, for example in primary education and access to healthcare. It would be extraordinary if there had not been, given the amount of money that has been spent on development in countries like Tanzania, Ghana, Rwanda and Uganda. But nowhere has the overall objective of nurturing the emergence of states that can take care of their own people without external assistance been met.

This emerges clearly from the statistics in Table 3.1, which shows an overwhelming upward trend in development assistance in the UK's priority countries. Over a ten-year period of delivering aid, in not one of these countries did DfID acknowledge success to the extent that it started to reduce its spending on the grounds that its developmental objectives had been achieved and that the recipient state was able to stand on its own feet. One of the few instances of a modest reduction in spending was Sierra Leone between 2004/05 and 2006/07. But DfID's programme budget in Sierra Leone none the less remained the highest per capita in Africa, and was set to jump back to a new high in 2007/08. Even in countries that DfID held up as examples of developmental success, Rwanda, Tanzania, Ghana and Mozambique, the amount of money the department spent just kept increasing.

Moreover, the upward trend in development assistance reflected in the table also shows that in not one of the UK's priority countries did DfID feel that it could admit *failure* and withdraw its assistance on the grounds that it was not achieving its developmental goals. Even in Zimbabwe, where the politics made it abundantly clear that the UK government could not possibly achieve any of its developmental objectives while Mugabe remained in power, DfID's budget kept increasing from £11 million in 1997/98 to £37 million in 2005/06. This was justified on humanitarian grounds. As Clare Short said: 'We have to feed them.' In Sudan, another country run by a government hostile to the UK's developmental and political agendas, DfID's spending increased from just over £5 million to almost £131 million between 2001/02 and 2005/06. This huge increase was justified on the grounds that it was required to support humanitarian operations and the 2005 Comprehensive Peace Agreement (CPA) between the government and the southern Sudanese rebels. Just as the money DfID spent in countries considered to be on the 'right' path kept increasing, so it did in the basket cases.

Weak states

If one sees the problem of Africa, as the British government and most donors do, as principally a problem of weak and failing states, then the problem looms very large indeed. Most African states are extremely problematic for Western policy-makers because they are either unable or unwilling to implement the political and economic reforms that donors believe are necessary for successful development to take place. From the donors' perspective, the challenge with such states is how to get them to the development starting line – the point at which African states themselves facilitate development by adopting and implementing sound policies rather than hinder it through corruption, predation and conflict. In Africa there are very few examples of states emerging as sound 'developmental' states, that is states with viable institutions capable of delivering security and economic advancement to their citizens. Where it has arguably happened, in South Africa, Mauritius and Botswana, for example, development assistance has either not been the determining factor, or has not been a factor at all in stimulating the transformation.

Traditionally Western policy-makers have seen themselves as confronted with a choice between three possible approaches to weak and failing states: ignore them, contain them, or fix them. In practice they have often shifted between all three options, depending on a range of factors including: their interests in the country in question; their relationship with its government; the complexity of the problems posed; the opportunities to effect change; and the perceived consequences of non-engagement. After the Americans' failed intervention in Somalia in 1993/94, there was a tendency on the part of the West to ignore really difficult states, and this contributed to the failure to intervene in Rwanda at that time. But Somalia demonstrated that ignoring a failed state could lead to adverse consequences down the line. Somalia's problems quickly became the problems of the whole region and the world: the country produced tens of thousands of refugees; it became a safe haven for Ethiopian rebels such as the Ogaden National Liberation Front and the Oromo Liberation Front; it harboured international terrorists; it hampered efforts to control the regional proliferation of small arms and light weapons; it became a nerve centre for commercial cattle rustling on a regional scale. These patterns were repeated in other parts of Africa, where the regional dimensions of failing to arrest state failure and conflict were becoming all too evident: in the Great Lakes, Zimbabwe, and the complex of conflicts in Sierra Leone, Liberia, Guinea and Côte d'Ivoire. After 9/11, it became clear that however difficult a country like Somalia or Afghanistan was to contain or to fix, it could not simply be ignored.

The second option of containment was essentially the policy adopted by the Labour government towards Zimbabwe and, at first, towards Sudan. In Zimbabwe, from about 1999 onwards, the UK government had come under increasing domestic pressure to take action against the regime of President Mugabe, even though the options were severely limited. In no other African crisis under Labour was there such sustained media and parliamentary interest, in part because of the commercial and historical ties between Zimbabwe and the UK, and in part because Mugabe adopted a deliberate policy of targeting white Zimbabwean farmers to shore up his own popularity and legitimacy. After twenty years of

Mugabe's misrule, Zimbabwe was by the late 1990s in deep economic and political trouble. By provoking the British over white farmers and land reform (legitimate sources of grievance for the majority of Zimbabweans), Mugabe created a distraction from his own corruption and misrule. The outspoken tone of British ministers, opposition politicians and the media on Zimbabwe, while morally justifiable, played into the hands of Mugabe, who accused the UK of post-colonial meddling. Meanwhile, the UK's efforts to put pressure on Zimbabwe through the Commonwealth and Southern African Development Community were frustrated by the reluctance of African elites to take a hard line against a fellow African leader and veteran of the struggle for independence. It is hard to see what an effective UK policy on Zimbabwe would look like. It is, however, significant that Blair at one point expressed his regret that military intervention in Zimbabwe was not politically feasible.[4]

In Sudan, another former British colony, the UK faced a completely different, and in many ways more challenging, set of problems. For the first half of the Blair era, Sudan appeared to British policy-makers to be another intractable African conflict, in fact one of the worst and most complex on the continent. In 1997 the chances of resolving the long-running civil war between the Khartoum government and the rebels of the Sudan People's Liberation Army (SPLA) seemed very distant. A more important priority was to contain the Islamist regime in Khartoum, which was seeking to spread its ideology and influence in the Horn of Africa and beyond. Another complicating factor for the British was that Sudan's oil, its Islamist regime and the evangelical Christian lobby in the United States (which was very committed to supporting the SPLA) meant that Washington was bound to be very much involved in any concerted international efforts to tackle Sudan. In 1998, after the al-Qaeda attacks on the US embassies in Nairobi and Dar es Salaam, President Clinton had ordered an attack on a Sudanese factory that Washington claimed was making ingredients for chemical weapons but which it seems was a *bona fide* pharmaceutical plant manufacturing nothing more harmful than aspirins.

After 9/11 the dynamics of the relationship between the West and Khartoum changed rapidly, presenting an opportunity for serious peace negotiations. The government had suffered a series of devastating setbacks in the war with the SPLA. It felt that unless it cooperated with Washington on a range of issues including counterterrorism it would, like the Taliban, be subject to military attack on account of its past association with al-Qaeda. And it wanted to enjoy the benefits of the revenue from the oil that was about to come on-stream without fear of Western interference and intervention. Offering a peace deal with the SPLA based on a promise of a referendum on independence for the south seemed like a small price to pay to avoid annihilation. The UK, along with the United States, Norway and Kenya, was in the forefront of the four years of tough negotiations that followed to secure agreement on a ceasefire, power and revenue sharing, and border demarcation. These led eventually to the signing of the CPA in January 2005.

The CPA was a remarkable achievement and one for which the UK can claim a lot of the credit. But it was not the end of the story. In 2003 another conflict in Sudan had come to the world's attention with the escalation of a low-level rebellion in Darfur, in the remote far west of the country. Like the war in the south, this crisis had its roots in the political and economic marginalization of peripheral regions and communities by the central government. The escalation may well have been prompted in part by the CPA itself, which in spite of its name was not an inclusive peace agreement. The Darfuris (along with some other Sudanese communities) were being excluded from a new power and revenue sharing dispensation and saw armed rebellion as the only way to claim a slice of the cake. Khartoum reacted to the rebellion with the same tactics it had used to such devastating effect in the south: by arming and providing logistical support to local proxy forces, militias recruited from local pastoralist communities, and setting them against the rebels and against the civilian communities that gave support and sustenance to the rebels. The inevitable result was a series of horrendous massacres and the destruction of villages and poisoning of wells throughout the region. This in turn quickly led to a major humanitarian catastrophe and the displacement of millions of people into camps within Darfur and across the border in Chad. Fearful that the crisis in Darfur would under-mine progress on the yet-to-be-signed CPA, the external archi-tects of the agreement, including the UK, failed to acknowledge the extent of the Darfur emergency, let alone put pressure on Khartoum to desist from policies that were leading to massive human rights abuses. As the leaders in Khartoum knew all too well, the extended time frame of CPA implementation was on their side. Highly priced oil was filling their coffers, increasing their power and their incentives to undermine the implementa-tion of the agreement at every step.

The UK's experience with Zimbabwe and Sudan under-lined the limits of Western policy options in the face of an un-cooperative weak state controlled by an abusive regime which is intent on remaining in power. In Liberia, however, the UK succeeded, with the help of the United States and its allies in the region, in getting rid of a non-cooperative government that was hampering progress in stabilizing both Liberia and the West African region. Liberia's president, Charles Taylor, was a warlord who had gained power through the ballot box in 1997, after a flawed UN and regionally brokered peace process. Once in power Taylor continued to rule much as he had as a rebellious warlord, through intimidation of his rivals at home and in the region, and through abusive economic exploitation. The UK was particularly alarmed by his persistent efforts to undermine the stability of Sierra Leone, where London was by 2000 investing money and effort in conflict resolution and where Taylor was continuing to foment rebellion. It therefore began to build a coalition of support within the region, internationally and among Liberian opposition groups to press for his removal from power and his indictment for war crimes by the Sierra Leone Special Court. It is worth noting that this strategy called for a paradoxical mixture of tools, including on the one hand a principled use of the evolving mechanisms of international criminal justice and on the other a pragmatic use of support for Liberian rebel groups opposed to Charles Taylor's regime. Eventually this effort succeeded and Taylor was first exiled to Nigeria and later arrested and extradited for trial at The Hague. Liberia now has a democratically elected president, Africa's only female head of state, Ellen Johnson Sirleaf, who is genuinely committed to working with the donors to put her country on the path of economic and political reform. The donors' approach had successfully shifted from seeking to contain to seeking to fix a failed state.

One problem with fixing failing states, the third option available to external actors faced with weak or failing states, is that the opportunity for the UN and others to move in with the kinds of remedies required often does not actually arise until the state has already collapsed or is on the verge of collapse. It is only an emergency, the perpetration of serious crimes against humanity, or a major threat to international security, which can legitimize and make politically feasible an external military intervention and full engagement in post-conflict state-building. One of the consequences of the failures of the United States and the UK in Iraq is that the bar for intervention has been significantly raised. What kind of a crisis would it take for the West to intervene in Africa now? Darfur and Zimbabwe continue to deteriorate without serious external action. Would the UK have intervened in Sierra Leone if the crisis there had emerged after 2001?

Sierra Leone is usually presented as the main example of successful UK intervention to rescue and fix a collapsed state. Indeed, since 2000 the UK has implemented a comprehensive strategy in Sierra Leone which addresses many of the political, economic, judicial, social and security problems facing a collapsed state. But it is possible to argue that, rather than addressing the root causes of state failure and conflict, and setting the country on the path to self-reliance, the UK strategy risks rebuilding a weak Sierra Leonean state vulnerable to future state failure and conflict. In particular, Sierra Leone today is still far from meeting the political and economic conditions identified by the UK and other donors as being essential for successful development. For so long as it fails to fulfil these conditions, Sierra Leone's continued viability will depend on a long-term UK commitment to guarantee its security and stability. One of the key lessons for the UK in Sierra Leone, repeated three years later in Iraq, was that the military campaign necessary to defeat the spoilers and stabilize the country is the easy part. The phase of 'post-conflict reconstruction' is very much more difficult. In fact, in failed African states such as Sierra Leone, Somalia and DR Congo 'reconstruction' is a misleading description, because it is not just a matter of rebuilding physical infrastructure, it is about rebuilding (or in fact in many cases building from scratch) viable political, social and economic institutions.

In the absence of a crisis of the kind that justified the UK intervention in Sierra Leone, the opportunities for engagement in addressing state weakness and failure are far more nuanced and constraining. In weak states that have not completely failed, or have managed to overcome or avoid civil conflict and collapse, the donors find themselves having to cut deals and reach agreements with weak but sovereign African states on development and reform packages designed to assist in addressing problems and getting those states to the point at which development assistance starts to 'work'. Most of the DfID's priority countries in Africa fall into this category. As noted, in such countries the development assistance of the UK and other donors have contributed to progress here and there. There is a constant risk, however, that progress will be undermined by shocks like conflict in neighbouring states, HIV, internal political threats, debt, collapse of commodity prices and natural disasters. Furthermore, as underlined above, the considerable investment by donors in nurturing the conditions they believe necessary for successful development has not yet put any of these weak African states unequivocally on the path to sustainable development and self-reliance.

A crucial problem in such states is the tension between the donors' eagerness to ensure that governments have 'ownership' of their development policies and the donors' understanding that without reasonable standards of governance development assistance is a waste of money. There is a danger that in their eagerness to hand over 'ownership' of their development programme to recipient governments, the donors underestimate or overlook the governance shortcomings that undermine development. The problem is exacerbated when the officials of donor governments come under pressure from their political masters to come up with 'good news' stories, quick wins and concrete deliverables, and to meet unrealistic performance targets.

Blunt instruments

As the UK has discovered through often difficult experience in Africa, the key to dealing with weak states is to identify where the donors' leverage lies and to apply it in effective ways. This is a very tricky task. Sometimes opportunities have been missed, as in Somalia, where there has been a reluctance to learn from the lessons of successful reconciliation in Somaliland. Sometimes pressure has been applied but turned out to be counter-productive, as occurred in Zimbabwe, where in truth very few real opportunities emerged in the ten years from 1997 to 2007. Sometimes, as the Sudan case showed, limited windows of opportunity emerged to effect change, but these led to new challenges which proved intractable. Sometimes opportunities were boldly grasped, as in Sierra Leone and Liberia, and, although the cost in terms of effort and resources was great, the benefits were tangible, at least in the initial stages of stabilization. Much of the time, however, and in much of Africa, it has simply been the case that the leverage of the UK government to secure its ultimate objective, the creation of developmental states, has been strictly limited.

In the absence of a genuine commitment on the part of a capable leadership to adopt sensible policies, and the institutional capacity to implement them transparently, donor assistance is not effective. But where neither the commitment nor the capacity is there, it is very hard for the foreign donors to conjure it up out of nothing. Almost always the leverage that donors have been able to bring to bear on African states is more limited than Western politicians believe. One reason for this is a lack of sound analysis and understanding on the part of donors of the cultural, political, economic and social contexts in which they are operating – the point made forcefully by the report of the Commission for Africa. African leaders, whether cooperative or antagonistic towards the West, tend to have a subtle understanding of the pressures under which Western politicians labour, and are often able to use this effectively to pursue agendas that sometimes directly contradict or undermine those of the donors. The donors themselves tend to be unable or unwilling to see through this dissimulation.

In most poor African countries money, in the form of large assistance programmes, debt relief, etc., does at least buy donors access to governments and a serious dialogue with them about development and governance. In some cases this has brought positive results. If you throw enough money at the primary education system you are bound eventually to get more children going to school, and likewise if you spend enough on rural health clinics, malaria and HIV prevention, then fewer people will die of preventable diseases. But the overarching aim of transforming states so that they stop hindering development and start facilitating it has always proved much more difficult. And the behaviour of the recipients of development assistance is constantly throwing up awkward questions and dilemmas for the donors. What happens, for example, when your development 'partner' in Africa starts to backslide on political and economic reforms? Or fiddles the accounts? Or locks up opposition leaders on trumped-up charges? Or threatens to undermine a painstakingly negotiated peace deal? Or changes the constitution to allow a president to run for a third term? Or invades a neighbouring country? And what of oil-rich poorly governed countries where development assistance represents a tiny fraction of national revenue?

The UK's mixed experience in Sierra Leone reveals just how elusive an external actor's leverage and influence can be, even in a context where a military presence and large economic commitment give that actor ostensible control over events and where international donor coordination is good. No threat to reduce the UK's commitment to Sierra Leone was credible as a means of applying leverage and it was never seriously contemplated. The UK's political investment in Sierra Leone's successful development was greater than that of many Sierra Leonean politicians, for whom corruption may be a necessary means of political survival and who therefore may have an interest in *unsuccessful* development. A large financial and political commitment brings pressure on the donor to disburse funds and to make sure the policy stays on the rails. That makes the donor dependent on the cooperation of the recipients of the assistance and gives the recipient some leverage over the donor. If even in Sierra Leone, for all its ability to control events and pressure the government, the UK faced these very difficult problems, then in more complex situations like Sudan and DR Congo, where the UK and other donors had far less leverage in the face of greater challenges, it was not surprising that the missions sometimes seemed impossible.

On paper (in the international objectives of the FCO, for example) the UK government recognizes the importance of political freedom and respect for human rights and the rule of law as essential ingredients for successful and sustainable economic development and political stability. In practice it has often found it particularly difficult to nurture political freedom and respect for human rights in states that are beneficiaries of UK aid but which are run by governments with a strong streak of authoritarianism. At times it has even appeared that the UK agrees with such governments when they argue that in order to maintain the control they need to bring about economic development they should be allowed to act in an authoritarian manner. This was certainly the reason for Clare Short's impatience with human rights activists' complaints about Rwanda's Paul Kagame. At any rate the UK, like other donors, has always found it very difficult to know what to do when African states to which it provides development assistance abuse human rights, undermine the rule of law, rig elections, curtail political freedoms or undermine regional stability by waging war against their neighbours. The UK has faced this dilemma in its relations with many of the countries in Africa that are recipients of significant quantities of UK aid. But the difficulties have been particularly acute in Uganda, Rwanda and Ethiopia.

Uganda and Rwanda have both committed egregious human rights abuses in DR Congo and have been involved in massive illegal exploitation of DR Congo's economic resources. At various times, the actions of Rwanda and Uganda have run counter to both UK interests and the stated principles of UK policy in DR Congo. Likewise Ethiopia has committed serious human rights abuses and violations of international humanitarian laws in Somalia and has defied the United Nations in its refusal to proceed to the demarcation of its border with Eritrea under the terms of the peace agreement that sought to bring an end to the border war between the two neighbours in 1998. Furthermore the governments of Ethiopia, Uganda and Rwanda have all engaged in serious abuses against their own citizens and have more or less blatantly rigged electoral processes in order to stay in power. The UK has sought to address these problems in various ways, through bilateral diplomatic pressure, through seeking to build international pressure, through threats to suspend aid, and sometimes even by temporarily withholding or reducing aid or channelling it in different ways. But in all cases the UK aid tap has remained firmly on, on the grounds that economic development and humanitarian action must take precedence and that the UK's investment in economic development in those countries must be safeguarded. Never has a strong message been sent to these or other governments about the benchmarks that need to be met and the standards of human rights that need to be maintained if they are to ensure a predictable flow of aid and to avoid seeing aid suspended or cut off. And this inevitably undermines the donors' leverage.

The donors – and the UK is no exception here – often have an exaggerated sense of the power of development assistance to effect change because they fail to recognize that most real development in Africa takes place in a rather different world from that imagined by Western development policy. For example, the donors have been impressed by the poverty reduction statistics in Uganda and Rwanda and have tended to credit their own development strategies for these successes. On those grounds DfID has stepped up its aid allocations to Uganda and Rwanda almost every year since 1997. But in both countries there is a real possibility that the impressive economic progress made from the late 1990s onwards has been due as much to the massive exploitation of the economic resources of DR Congo by the Ugandan and Rwandan governments under the cover of security operations there as to the development assistance of the donors. In Tanzania progress on poverty reduction in spite of large injections of donor assistance has been widely recognized as sluggish. Nevertheless, there has been significant economic growth. But this is driven more by the expansion of the extractive industries sector than by donor assistance. Likewise, the impressive growth figures in Sudan since 1999 are entirely due to oil production. Indeed, in oil-producing states like Sudan, Angola and Nigeria the donors' development efforts are all but irrelevant because of the vast oil wealth at the disposal of the elites who hold the levers of power and decision-making. The competition for contracts among donors also takes the edge off any leverage there might be. In such resource-rich countries development and humanitarian assistance becomes at best a not very important pawn in the diplomatic games elites play with the Europeans, the Americans and other donors. At worst it is just another resource to exploit in order to consolidate power. In Nigeria DfID tried in vain to find a 'development strategy' that worked, that actually dented the very high poverty figures. But repeated failures did not prevent the UK from increasing its bilateral spend in Nigeria from £6 million to £80 million between 1997 and 2005, or from signing off on the Paris Club's multi-billion-dollar debt relief deal with Nigeria.

One potential solution to the problem of limited leverage is to try to help build strong institutions that can protect states and regions from the abuses of individual leaders or cliques. The question is which institutions should be strengthened: those of the state itself or those of civil society? The answer is probably both. Much can be done to strengthen states through grounding them firmly in the rule of law and respect for human rights: building the capacity of the judiciary; reform and education of the military and police forces; constitutional reform, etc. There is also useful work that can be done in building the capacity of regional and subregional organizations to prevent, resolve and manage conflicts. As noted already, the UK itself has been a pioneer in many of these institutional capacity-building approaches at state and regional levels. But the weakness of this approach is that unless it is done exceptionally carefully and with a full appreciation of specific political contexts, it risks strengthening the state without reforming it, perpetuating political elites and their rent-seeking bureaucracies, and marginalizing those elements in society with the greatest energy and motivation to effect positive transformation.

In Sierra Leone the UK adopted a Manichaean attitude to the conflict: Kabbah's was a 'democratically elected government'; the rebels were, in Blair's words, 'gangsters' and 'terrorists'.[5] But for all their many faults, the rebels did represent the real grievances of many ordinary Sierra Leoneans against three generations of political leaders. Sierra Leone's political elite bore the greatest responsibility for creating the conditions for state failure and conflict. 'They stole our diamonds, they stole our gold,' went the anthem of the rebel Revolutionary United Front, referring to the corruption of successive Sierra Leonean governments. And it was true. After the British intervention, the symptoms of the conflict were squarely addressed: the rebels were disarmed and their leaders prosecuted; security was established; and the British embarked on a massive programme of reform, including the reform of political and judicial institutions and of the army and police. This certainly had very real benefits for the majority of people in Sierra Leone. But at the same time the political power of the elite was reinforced on the basis of massive infusions of UK development assistance channelled through their hands and failure to address the problem of corruption. Contained within this corruption were the seeds of future resentment and conflict. In July 2007 a leading NGO predicted that 'the population's tolerance of bad governance and lack of economic development is unlikely to last much longer'. Unless this was addressed 'a return to conflict would become a real possibility'.[6]

The shortcomings of top-down approaches are also evident in the peace processes in Sudan, Somalia and DR Congo. In Sudan the Comprehensive Peace Agreement between the north and the south, while making rhetorical nods towards the need for greater political participation, has ended up reinforcing the authoritarianism of both the rebels and the government. The CPA does envisage elections in 2008/09, but even if they go ahead the chances of them leading to the formation of a democratic government respectful of the rights of its citizens in the north or in the south (let alone in the whole country) are remote. And yet, as noted above, the failure to ensure inclusiveness has already contributed to continuing conflict in Sudan. In Somalia the insistence of external actors on dealing with the warlords and faction leaders while excluding clan elders and representatives of civil society from having an effective voice in negotiations has contributed to the failure of one peace process after another. In DR Congo the peace process has equally ended up being a process of power sharing between warlords and rapacious elites, thus risking re-creating exactly the same kind of weak-state dynamics that led to the conflict in the first place. In response to these criticisms, the UK government argues that genuinely inclusive peace agreements to end such conflicts are simply too difficult to achieve in the short term, but that in the longer term such agreements, backed up by properly funded post-conflict reconstruction, could provide a space and a catalyst for more inclusive politics.

This may be true, but the experience of civil society, even in African states that have avoided such devastating conflicts, is not always encouraging. In these states lip-service is certainly paid to the need for wider political participation in the Poverty Reduction Strategy Papers now required of low-income countries as a condition for debt relief and donor finance for development. The EU, NEPAD, the AU and the subregional African organizations also call for the participation of civil society in assessing development needs and formulating development strategies. But when it comes to implementation of these policies there is a big gap between rhetoric and reality. The UK itself talks about the importance of civil society but actually spends a small fraction of its programme budget in Africa supporting civil society.[7] African governments are rarely willing to allow civil society to participate except on their own terms, and donors are reluctant to push them for fear of further weakening weak states. The fear is not without justification. It can be argued that the bottom-up approach of nurturing self-reliance at the community level also brings serious risks of stimulating exactly the centrifugal and ethnically divisive forces that have nurtured conflict and undermined states in the past.

Contradictions and dilemmas

The UK's leverage in Africa was also undermined by the contradictions between the UK's very public and direct commitment to poverty reduction and the more discreet and indirect commitment to promoting and protecting the UK's strategic, commercial and economic interests identified in the last chapter. DfID may have explicitly untied British development aid from British commercial interests, but, as has been noted, this did not mean that commercial, economic and strategic interests were banished from UK foreign policy deliberations. In addition to the common interests that united Africa and the donors there were also uncommon interests which, unless managed carefully, could divide them.

Whitehall did not send a strong message to British business to deter involvement in abusive exploitation of resources and labour in Africa. Nor did it show enthusiasm for regulatory measures that would make it harder for UK businesses to get involved in or facilitate the abusive exploitation of African resources and workers. London pointedly neglected to investigate the allegations made in a 2002 report by the UN that a number of prominent UK companies were involved in the illegal exploitation of the economic resources of DR Congo. There was more embarrassment for the UK in 2004 when it came to light that a number of rich UK expatriates and residents, including Mark Thatcher, the son of the former British prime minister, were involved in a conspiracy to overthrow the government of Equatorial Guinea. The tiny state of Equatorial Guinea had recently become the focus of attention for international oil companies because of the discovery of huge oil reserves. It was also one of the most corrupt countries in Africa, run by a government with a terrible human rights record and with a history of internecine plots and counterplots within the ruling family. The alleged plot came to light when a plane carrying arms and mercenaries, led by an old Etonian called Simon Mann, was impounded at Harare airport en route to Equatorial Guinea. Mann was arrested, charged with illegal exportation of weapons and immigration offences and imprisoned. Other alleged plotters were arrested and imprisoned in Equatorial Guinea itself. Thatcher himself was arrested and charged in South Africa. He admitted his role in the plot under a plea bargain and avoided a prison term. In spite of the involvement of a number of British nationals and residents in the case, there was no move by the UK to investigate the allegations.

Tony Blair himself, for all his commitment to poverty reduction in Africa, was hard nosed when it came to protecting British business interests on the continent, including those of the UK's military industries, even when they risked undermining development. Clare Short, after her resignation as Secretary of State for International Development, was scathing about the double standards of both the FCO and Number 10 in this respect. The FCO, she said, allowed its concern to help British Airways get a contract with the corrupt Angolan government for scheduled flights to Luanda undermine her department's efforts to overcome obstacles thrown up by the Angolan government on humanitarian assistance to millions of needy Angolans at the end of the war.[8] She was particularly infuriated by Blair's refusal in 2002 to stop a major BAE deal to provide Tanzania with a £28 million military air-traffic control system which many, including Blair's own development officials and the World Bank, said was both unnecessary and beyond Tanzania's means. This was, according to Short, one clear occasion when the prime minister was asked unambiguously to choose between what was good for poor Africans and what was good for British industry. He chose the latter. Arms sales were, said Short, 'Tony's blind spot'.[9] It was a blind spot that led in 2007 to the suspension of the Serious Fraud Office's investigation into the alleged payment over many years of billions of pounds of bribes and kickbacks in relation to BAE's multi-billion-pound Yamamah arms contract with Saudi Arabia, a scandal which seriously undermined the UK government's ability to speak to African governments with clear moral authority on the crucial issue of governance and corruption.

After 9/11 even more acute contradictions emerged between the UK government's counterterrorism policies (including its involvement in Iraq) and its objectives to nurture good governance, development and stability in Africa. There were a number of different factors at play here. First, as has been noted in the last chapter, the United States and the UK started to build alliances with African states that were based on cooperation in counterterrorism as much as, or more than, on cooperation in achieving good governance, conflict resolution and economic development. Sudan was an interesting example. The Khartoum regime's fear that it would be a military target after 9/11 because of its Islamist ideology and connections to al-Qaeda led it to offer deep cooperation with the United States on what it knew about terrorist networks. The new relationship, together with the eagerness of the Khartoum elite to enjoy the country's new oil revenues, created a diplomatic opening that allowed the United States and the UK to push for a north–south peace deal. But later, when the US/UK strategy in the Middle East began to backfire following the invasion of Iraq, the likelihood of US military action against Sudan was removed. Khartoum was then in a much better position to use its own leverage with Washington on intelligence issues to deflect pressure from the USA and the EU to end its abusive practices in Darfur, to move towards a more inclusive and democratic form of governance, to implement its obligations under the north–south peace agreement, and to cooperate with the International Criminal Court's investigations into war crimes in Darfur.

Another example was Ethiopia, a much more willing partner in counterterrorism, which was able to use to great advantage its role as an indispensable ally in a region where Islamic extremism was seen to be growing. Ethiopia was thus able to resist pressure to implement the terms of its peace agreement with Eritrea, to deflect criticism of its violent suppression of the political opposition following the 2005 elections, and to engage in a violent regional campaign to annihilate its own rebel groups under the cover of counterterrorism operations in Somalia. During this period, even though DfID did shift its aid to Ethiopia away from direct budget support after 2005, the UK's overall aid budget to Ethiopia increased quite considerably. Across Africa, counterterrorism concerns led to a deepening of the relationships between Western and African security and intelligence agencies. This in turn resulted in a distinct militarization of the

West's approach to African states, which served to strengthen the very groups whose actions and lack of accountability had been the cause of so much conflict and destabilization in Africa in the past.

The second problem with the counterterrorism approach to Africa adopted by the UK, the United States and their allies was that it risked radicalizing new potential enemies of the West even as it sought to eliminate the existing ones. Across the Muslim world, including in Africa, the hardline counterterrorism policies of the United States and the UK, the short-sighted policies pursued in Iraq, Palestine, Lebanon and Somalia, and the conflation of all stripes of political Islam with terrorism have not only badly damaged the reputations of the UK and the United States. They have also helped to marginalize Islamist moderates and have played into the hands of extremists, winning them more sympathy and recruits from the poor and the dispossessed. It is hard to predict what impact these developments will have on the achievement of the UK's wider political and economic objectives in Africa. But in a continent where many countries have mixed Muslim and Christian populations, and where Christian fundamentalism is also on the rise, the perception of an emerging conflict between the West and political Islam is likely to be destabilizing. Ethiopia's war in Somalia in 2006/07 has inevitably been presented by the Islamists in quasi-religious terms. But there have also been signs of increasing political tensions between Muslims and Christians in Kenya, Uganda, Nigeria and within Ethiopia itself.

Third, although the UK itself ramped up its aid to Africa in the aftermath of 9/11, security concerns radically transformed the international context in which decisions on development aid and poverty reduction were made. The war in Iraq cost the UK government about a billion pounds a year between 2003 and 2007. Afghanistan cost the government over a billion in the same period. DfID itself increased its spending in Afghanistan from almost nothing in 2001/02 to about £100 million in 2005/06, and in Pakistan from £42 million to £71 million in the same period. Both programmes were set to increase in 2007/08. Meanwhile in Africa DfID's programme in Somalia increased from less than £2 million in 2001/02 to almost £19 million in 2005/06. Although these increases could be justified in terms of poverty reduction, there is little doubt that they were also motivated by security concerns. These large increases both in military spending and in 'security-related' development spending raise some worrying questions. Will donors start to divert aid from poverty reduction to counterterrorism goals? Will debts incurred to fight insurgencies in Iraq, Afghanistan and elsewhere start to eat away at aid budgets? And will security concerns make it even more difficult for donors to pursue coordinated aid policies than in the past?

Finally, because UK diplomats and embassies were increasingly seen as potential targets of terrorism, security fears meant that after 9/11 UK diplomats were retreating ever farther behind high compound walls and security perimeters. In some cases embassies were physically moved out of the centre of capital cities into the suburbs, close to the villas of the elites but far removed from the reality of life in the countries they were supposedly reporting on. Strict rules were imposed on travel outside the embassy or residential areas. Sometimes whole districts were put out of bounds for official travel, or, in the case of Somalia, a whole country. Such measures, while understandable as necessary to reduce threats to staff, none the less also reduced the capacity of the UK government to provide the detailed analysis and reporting that are essential ingredients for sound decision- and policy-making and for navigating the complex dilemmas of politics, conflict and development in Africa.

Technocrats and diplomats

It was not just concerns about security which were reducing the government's ability to understand and report on events in Africa. DfID's ascendancy on African issues came at the cost of a significant decline in the FCO's diplomatic and analytical capacity in Africa. DfID was a new department without baggage which came to symbolize the new altruism and ambition of the Labour government's policies in Africa. It grew in confidence with the resources that were thrown at it. New DfID offices were opened in Africa and they were filled with advisers, technical experts and coordinators. But in the same period the FCO suffered a serious crisis of identity and purpose, worsened by the diplomatic disasters of Blair's policies in the Middle East. In Whitehall as well as in the media people asked what the FCO was for in the twenty-first century. Did the UK need so many expensive embassies – and diplomats – around the world? Reviews were undertaken and it was decided that the FCO needed to focus more on cross-cutting themes such as terrorism, failed states and climate change, and less on individual countries, unless these were considered to be of paramount importance. Accordingly the FCO embarked on a major restructuring. In the very year that Tony Blair declared to be the year of Africa, 2005, the FCO's directorate responsible for Africa was forced to slash its budget – closing embassies in Swaziland, Madagascar and Lesotho, amalgamating country desks and offering early retirement to analysts. The minister responsible for Africa at the FCO was unable to fight Africa's corner in Whitehall – the job did not have enough clout and changed hands five times in the ten years from 1997 to 2007.

Of course, these trends did not mean that the UK's policy in Africa – a policy aimed at achieving what is a fundamentally political goal of nurturing states capable of delivering economic development to their people – was being designed and implemented without regard to politics, diplomacy and intelligence. Clare Short, in her memoir of her time in the cabinet, says that she persuaded the Secret Intelligence Service, which technically falls under the FCO, to carry out intelligence-gathering operations on behalf of DfID that would help the new department in its development efforts.[10] Over its first decade in existence DfID became more aware of the need for development actors to get their hands dirty with politics, as a DfID policy paper on governance and development published in 2007 made clear.

> A major challenge for all donors – bilateral and multilateral – is how to engage with power. Our understanding of governance has broadened and deepened significantly over the past decade. It has gone beyond economic governance and the management of the economy, and beyond analysing and reforming public services and the public sector. The focus is now about how power is used, and on whose behalf. Governance work has moved away from asking 'What is wrong and how we can fix it?' to asking 'What are the incentives to which political elites respond and how can they be changed?' Asking these sorts of questions makes our work both more relevant but also more challenging. It takes us into the heart of politics and how political systems work, and whether or not they benefit poor people.[11]

But while DfID knew what the problems were, it did not have the political and diplomatic capacity required to deliver the solutions. Development ideology and institutional interests led to good advice being ignored or downplayed. Technical expertise, objective-setting and the implementation of 'logical frameworks' were valued above knowledge and analysis of realities on the ground. Instead of posing the problems of development in political terms and proposing political solutions, DfID posed the problems in technical terms and proposed technical solutions – often in the form of capacity-building. While it was becoming increasingly fashionable to pay lip-service to Africa's immense diversity, the technical approach to problem-solving in DfID created institutional pressure to find what 'worked' and 'scale it up', regardless of local differences within countries or across the continent. There was not enough critical examination and assessment either of the aims of UK development policy (were they realistic, achievable?) or of the leverage and influence that the British were able to bring to bear to achieve those aims. In its endeavours DfID, following development fashion, described – and genuinely sought to regard – the governments that were recipients of development assistance as 'partners' who should be encouraged in some way to have 'ownership' of development programmes and frameworks that were mostly designed by non-Africans without sufficient regard to the diverse political realities on the ground. There was little effort on the part of UK development policy-makers to put themselves in the position of their African development partners or to imagine what ownership of these policies might really mean to them.

Furthermore, for all the rhetoric about lesson learning and evaluation, there was little historical perspective in the Labour government's approach to Africa. DfID, like Blair and Brown, tended to look at Africa as a blank sheet on which for the first time the UK was inscribing a splendid and ambitious design. Brown surprised many historians when he said on a visit to Africa in 2005 that Britain had no need to apologize for its colonial history in Africa. That was not how Africans saw it. They remembered the suppression of Mau Mau in Kenya and the Devlin Commission's report into Britain's 'police state' colony in Nyasaland in the 1950s. Britain, which in its time had been the predominant colonial power in Africa, had a long and sometimes ugly history in Africa. Both in the colonial and the post-colonial period rhetoric about bringing civilization and economic development to the continent had jostled with the naked pursuit of British political and economic interests, often to the detriment of Africans themselves. Africans were entitled to ask whether there was anything new in the post-1997 Labour government's approach.

The British taxpaying public and media largely seemed to go along with the narrative of UK policy in Africa presented by the government. In an age of distrust of politicians, Blair and Brown's policy of increasing aid to poor Africans was one thing the puplic felt good about, in part because of the celebrity hype that surrounded it. There was little criticism or even scrutiny of Labour's developmental approach to Africa. But there were pertinent questions that the British public and media should have been asking of their government. It was less than half a century since a British government had precipitously begun to abandon an Africa that it knew exceptionally well as the leading colonial power after concluding that it lacked the resources required to maintain its African empire in the face of growing nationalist pressure. Now here was a British government embarking on a huge and costly programme of conflict resolution and economic development in a continent of which it had comparatively little detailed contemporary knowledge or understanding. Was the public's worthy angst about the tragic state of Africa being channelled into an effort that was actually working? Was it really true, as the government often claimed, that the UK had such pressing national interests in pursuing an interventionist development policy in Africa? And if it was true, what would be the consequences for the UK of the failure of its efforts to reduce poverty and bring economic development to Africa?

4 | Futures

The longer Blair stayed in office, the more interested he became in foreign policy, a trend that affects many second- and third-term leaders. As Blair himself once said, his motivation for going into politics was to make a difference in the world. But making a difference in an economically successful democracy is not an easy task. There is much political and policy detail to take in. A lot of unruly and ungrateful but powerful constituencies and lobbying groups need to be persuaded and brought on board: trade unions, business, civil servants, NGOs, media barons and so on. If a prime minister messes up, he or she pays for it in the polls. And if the machinery of government is already functioning well at home, delivering tolerably efficient services, economic opportunities and security at a reasonable cost to the taxpayer, many people don't actually want their leaders to make that much of a difference if that means constant interference. Domestic policy, then, is a hard slog with little reward. Foreign policy, on the other hand, provides a much more promising canvas, especially for a 'big picture' man like Blair. The potential to make a difference seems far greater in poor or poorly governed countries such as many of those in Africa. The international statesman needs only to focus on the grand strategy. If there is scope for military action then so much the better: commands are obeyed and the results can be immediate and spectacular. The complex political detail can be left to local actors. If things go well there is much credit to be won both at home and on the international stage. If they go badly, it is always possible to blame the 'spoilers' or the 'extremists' or the incompetence and corruption of allies.

Blair was lucky in his first major foreign adventures. The almost forgotten Desert Fox episode was successfully spun as a first Blair victory in the sparring with Iraq's Saddam Hussein. In Kosovo Blair brought a reluctant President Clinton around to military action against Slobodan Milosevic, stared down the sceptics, held his nerve and ended up winning the approval of liberal interventionists and hawks alike. Blair's deployment of British troops to Sierra Leone looked like an even greater political risk and for much less strategic gain. It was a purely humanitarian intervention in a distant tropical African country where the UK had no important interests. But it paid off. The decision to intervene rescued the UN from what would have been another peacekeeping disaster and boosted the UK's and Blair's reputation in Africa and beyond. Success in conflict resolution was matched by new approaches to economic development in Africa and elsewhere in which the UK took a leading role. Freed from the strategic constraints of the cold war, it was hoped that overseas assistance would be channelled into creating the political conditions for genuine economic development. Though the UK underestimated the difficulties of this challenge, at least it sought to engage in addressing the tricky problems of governance and conflict.

Blair's success overseas in his first term in office, together with his frustration at being unable to push through a radical reform programme at home, fed his ambitions in foreign affairs. He began to see himself as a latter-day William Gladstone with a mission to make the world a better place. Then history came along in the form of the attacks on the United States by al-Qaeda and gave Blair a chance to elevate the mission to the level of urgent national and global imperative. Not only *should* the world be reordered. It *had to be* if the extremism that found such spectacular expression on 11 September 2001 in New York City was to be dealt with. 9/11 therefore made possible and necessary what

Blair was already seeking to achieve. The military campaigns in Afghanistan and Iraq were the most dramatic instances of the effort to use 9/11 as an opportunity to 'reorder the world', as Blair himself put it in his first speech after 9/11. But Blair was also drawn to fixing Africa's problems: solving conflicts, strengthening states and catalyzing economic development. First he was drawn to it because he thought it was possible and because he saw it as a moral mission worthy of his own Christian values. Then, after 9/11, the mission was harnessed to the more urgent task of combating extremism. 'The state of Africa', Blair said in 2001, 'is a scar on the conscience of the world. But if the world as a community focused on it, we could heal it. And if we don't, it will become deeper and angrier.'[1]

The post-9/11 world was more amenable to Blair's black-and-white view of international politics than the messy world of small, unconnected conflicts which emerged in the immediate aftermath of the cold war. Rhetorically Blair merged the political violence in Iraq, Afghanistan, Pakistan, Lebanon, Palestine, London, the Balkans and Africa into one global conflict, and, he argued, it was a conflict that it was essential to win. But in reality, in Africa as elsewhere, 9/11 did not change much. In the continent's worst-ever war, in DR Congo, people died in the same numbers and for the same reasons the day after 9/11 as they did the day before. This was the kind of terrorism that mattered to most Africans. The conflicts were real enough. But they were not part of Blair's global and existential conflict.

Furthermore, while 9/11 may have acted as a stimulus on the UK government to devote more attention and resources to Africa's economic development, it also led the UK, and the Americans, to adopt counterterrorism strategies in the Middle East and in Africa which, it has been argued in this book, risked undermining international development efforts in Africa and weakened the capacity and the leverage of the United States and the UK to bring about the kinds of changes they believed necessary to transform African states. Viewed from one perspective there was a return to a cold war type of paradigm in which strategic concerns – now the fear was about the spread of political Islam rather than of Soviet influence – once more took precedence over concerns about economic development, governance and human rights. From another perspective there was a return to a more colonial mentality. Though on a lesser scale and with far fewer resources than in Afghanistan and Iraq, in Africa's unstable regions UK and US decision-makers were engaged, under the guise of partnership with African governments, in a quasi neo-imperialist project in which the quest to secure trade, investment and energy interests was tied up with grandiose plans to bring about stability through political transformation and state-building. But as in Iraq and Afghanistan, neither the UK nor the United States had the drive, the commitment and the self-belief that their colonial forebears could bring to the task. And even if individuals like Blair felt they did, their publics, world opinion and the populations of states they were seeking to transform were not convinced.

So what is the balance sheet of the first ten years of British policy in Africa under Labour? Four big new ideas and approaches to Africa for which the Blair government can claim some credit stand out: the idea of enhanced partnership with African governments committed to good governance and poverty reduction; the idea of a massive increase in donor assistance to Africa in order to kick-start economic development and eliminate poverty; the idea of military intervention to rescue failed states; and the idea of harnessing celebrity humanitarianism to a UK-led international effort to stimulate political and economic regeneration in Africa.

At a pan-African level the idea of enhanced partnership (as envisaged by Blair) did not survive the negotiations between the donors and African governments over the establishment of the New Partnership for African Development. Nevertheless, the UK government did pursue the same model in its bilateral dealings with a number of African states that it regarded as 'good performers'. This was a bold approach which involved banking on the quite sensible idea that aid is most efficiently spent when it is pledged over a long timeframe to governments that use it to support their own development strategies. It is too early to say with confidence that the approach has either succeeded or failed. There have been some setbacks, most notably when DfID felt it had to suspend direct budget support to Ethiopia after the government there violently clamped down on the opposition in the aftermath of the 2005 elections. On the other hand DfID's strategy has allowed the UK to engage in and influence a serious and practical debate on economic development with its selected African partners. The underlying weakness of the approach is that it puts too much faith in Africa's political elites and not enough in the genuine forces of progress and democracy that are to be found in African society.

The big UK push for increased donor assistance to Africa has also seen mixed results. The donors' pledges on aid and debt relief have been quite impressive. Much of this was due to Blair's persistent work on Africa at successive G8 summits and elsewhere. But the gap between promises and delivery remains wide. Furthermore, even though most of the key players in the UK government recognized that increased investment and trade were likely to be much more effective ways of unlocking economic development in Africa, they allowed aid and debt to grab the headlines for political reasons: they knew pledges on aid and debt were easier to extract from the other donors than substantial progress on trade and investment. Thus political considerations helped to skew the agenda towards aid, leading to a rapid bloating of the UK's aid budget without enough consideration being given to how the money could be effectively and strategically spent. By 2007 DfID was struggling to find good ways of spending all the extra money it had been given by the Treasury.

The UK's military operation in Sierra Leone in 2000 put humanitarian military action back on the West's agenda for the first time since the failure of the US intervention in Somalia in 1993. Furthermore, the success of the operation sent a message that rippled across Africa's conflict zones about the political will of a Western nation to come to the rescue of a floundering UN peacekeeping force and a failed state threatened with anarchy. This was accompanied by considerable progress in building African and UN capacity to conduct effective peacekeeping operations in Africa. The military phase of the UK's intervention in Sierra Leone worked out well both for the British government and for the Sierra Leoneans. Nevertheless, after its intervention the UK government 'owned' the problem of Sierra Leone. After 2000 fixing the problem of Sierra Leone (a relatively unimportant and small country) sucked up a disproportionate quantity of UK resources available for conflict management in Africa. Seven years on, the UK still has not shifted ownership of the problem of Sierra Leone to the Sierra Leone government. Moreover, the military interventions in Afghanistan and Iraq, seen as far more important by the UK government than anything it ever contemplated in Africa, soon banished the prospect of further direct UK military operations south of the Sahara.

The fourth big idea of Labour was also the most difficult to assess: the exploitation of celebrity humanitarianism to promote its Africa policy. Of course celebrity humanitarianism was not entirely the work of the UK government, but from 1997 to 2007 Blair did more than any other Western leader to tap into and encourage the interest of celebrities in raising the profile of Africa and in putting pressure on the rich world to do more to help solve its problems. This strategy did at least help to put Africa firmly on the international agenda. But it also tended to oversimplify popular perceptions of highly complex problems. This led to pressures that distorted the policy agenda in favour of actions and measures that were not necessarily the most effective ones and which could even be counterproductive. Moreover, celebrity humanitarianism lifted the public debate on Africa on to a highly emotive intellectual level where it became increasingly difficult to ask the necessary tough questions about Western policies and about accountability for the way aid was spent.

The signs are that Africa will remain an important foreign policy priority under Gordon Brown, the new prime minister, and that the direction of UK policy will, in the short term, remain the same. Brown's agenda in Africa includes more aid (he has floated the idea of a Marshall Plan for Africa); a big push on education (which he believes to be a powerful driver of change); a sustained focus on poverty reduction (with an accent on reducing child poverty); debt relief and debt cancellation; more action on reducing trade barriers; and sustained work to tackle corruption, for example through pushing the Extractive Industries Transparency Initiative. Having bankrolled the creation and expansion of DfID, and hobnobbed for a decade with the great and the good of the international aid bureaucracy, Brown is if anything even more politically committed than his predecessor to the notion that foreign policy goals can be achieved through social and economic development. At the same time the cuts Brown demanded at the FCO when he was Chancellor indicate that he is not particularly concerned by the government's diminishing capacity to report and analyse the political complexities and realities that challenge that notion. But if he really wants to be a player in Africa, Brown will be forced to get his hands dirty with the day-to-day politics of the continent: the conflicts and peace processes, the difficult trade-offs between counterterrorism and development, development and governance, governance and energy security, and so on. As much as pre-laid plans and programmes, it will be events, and how the Brown government reacts to them, which will determine its policies.

In the medium term some kind of course correction in UK policy towards Africa is probably unavoidable. The contradictions and dilemmas outlined in this book between Africa's economic development and the West's commercial and strategic interests have been greatly exacerbated by the United States' insistence on seeing Africa mainly through the lenses of energy security and the 'war on terror'. These contradictions urgently need to be addressed. There are also signs that the Africans themselves are growing tired of the development approaches of the UK and other donors. The failure of foreign aid to deliver tangible results and its tendency to promote humiliating dependence are increasingly irksome for Africans. The insistence of Western leaders like Blair that they know what is best for Africa and that Africans must choose 'the right path' if they are to get Western support causes much resentment. There are already signs of a backlash in the attitude of 'difficult' African states.

Then there is Iraq. While Brown will no doubt want to distance himself from the more glaring foreign policy blunders of the Blair government, he will none the less have to address the consequences of those mistakes: a more unstable Middle East, an unresolved crisis with Iran, a resurgence of political Islam, loss of UK and US influence in the Muslim world and beyond, and increasing pressures on aid budgets. Many of those consequences, together with emerging challenges related to the increasing economic and political influence of China, dwindling energy reserves and climate change, will affect the UK's ability to pursue its ambitious policy objectives in Africa effectively. Whether under Brown or under a future Conservative government, a readjustment of the UK's strategy to achieve those objectives and even a reformulation of the objectives themselves may therefore become necessary as the UK's perception of the balance of its interests in Africa evolves.

So what of the longer-term prognosis? The first ten years of Labour's government coincided with a period of extraordinary economic growth. If transferring money from the rich world to the poor was the right solution to the problems of poverty and underdevelopment in Africa, then this was the best of times to implement it. Never before had so much surplus wealth been available in the rich world to help the poor. As the Commission for Africa put it, the world was 'awash with wealth'. As long as it was just a question of giving money, the will was there among the public to give some of it to Africa. What was missing, however, was the will of the governments of most rich countries (the UK was among the most generous) to make the hard political decisions necessary to deliver on their promises with regard to aid, trade and debt relief. The pledges on aid and debt that Blair extracted from the G8 leaders at Gleneagles in 2005 were an impressive demonstration of his powers of persuasion. He had honed his moral arguments in the report of the Commission for Africa. But two years later these pledges remained largely unmet. None of the ambitious targets on aid and debt had been reached. On trade, where the commitments had been less generous, the negotiations at the World Trade Organization consistently failed to live up to the demands of those who felt that Africa's chance lay not with massive transfers of cash but with greater and fairer access to the markets of the industrialized world. Two years after Gleneagles the best that the rich world was offering the poor was 'the usual mercantilist stitch-up with the great powers seeking to extract as many concessions as they can while giving the bare minimum in return'.[2]

Some economists believe that the current period of economic growth will continue. As evidence they point to the fact that rising energy prices have not led to economic recession as in the past. Furthermore, optimists believe that carbon energy reserves are sufficient to ensure a smooth transition to the use of alternative sources of energy, thus avoiding any shocks associated with climate change. In this scenario decision-makers in donor states such as the UK will have the luxury of continuing their current efforts to leverage greater aid and debt relief for Africa and gradually to reduce the trade barriers that are such a formidable obstacle to Africa's economic development. This, of course, will not automatically lead to improvements in Africa. As the UK and other donors now recognize, without addressing governance and armed conflict, no amount of aid will unlock a brighter future for much of Africa.[3] But at least there is a chance that if the global economic system remains fundamentally solid the UK's proposed solutions will work and the ambitious task the UK has set itself can be followed through. The results are unlikely to be spectacular, but there may be some modest improvements over time.

These optimistic assumptions, however, are not universally shared. What if the scenario of continued economic growth proves to be plain wrong and the economic underpinnings of the current boom begin to falter? Peak oil theorists believe that oil reserves will start to run out much earlier than oil industry officials forecast, perhaps as early as the beginning of the next decade. This would lead to further, more dramatic, oil price hikes and serious global economic recession. Africa would be particularly vulnerable because such a recession would reduce the high prices for its commodities which have underpinned recent growth. Further deterioration of the political situation in the Middle East, for example the escalation of the crisis in relations between the West and Iran, could exacerbate the energy crisis and undermine the confidence of financial markets. But even without higher oil prices, interest rate increases could create a credit squeeze and trigger large losses on financial markets. And climate change and other environmental crises may cause unforeseen shocks that demonstrate what many experts are now beginning to fear: that the high levels of economic growth on which the current global economic system is based are ecologically unsustainable. In some combination of any of these adverse economic circumstances the approach to Africa of a major donor such as the UK, and indeed of all the major external players in Africa, including China, would be certain to undergo a serious change. The political pressures for greater trade protectionism would increase. International competition for Africa's natural resources would sharpen. Aid budgets for Africa would be diverted or dry up just as Africa began to suffer a new cycle of decline owing to a combination of the continuing failure of the donors' development policies to strengthen states through governance reform and renewed conflicts over resources and pressures associated with climate change.

Even if the storm clouds ahead are not as heavy as those forecast in this worst-case scenario, the UK and other donors face a serious dilemma. On the one hand it is recognized that instability, conflict, poor governance and poverty in Africa and other parts of the world are exacerbating some of the most serious challenges faced by our societies, including international terrorism, crime and migration. On the other hand those very challenges, in addition to climate change and dwindling energy resources, generate political pressure for short-term measures that can undermine efforts to achieve development, poverty reduction and conflict resolution in the most difficult parts of the world. Furthermore, even in the most favourable of circumstances it is not clear that the donors' current prescriptions for economic development in weak and failing states are working. As the pressures exerted by this dilemma on UK and other Western policy-makers increase, the gap between the principles of liberal intervention, underpinned by human rights, the rule of law and humanitarianism, and the perceived imperatives of self-interest will grow wider. Already this is evident in Western policies in Iraq, Afghanistan and the Middle East. In Africa it is most obvious in the donors' policies towards Somalia and Darfur.

Closing that gap should be the main priority of UK foreign policy. Upholding liberal principles may not guarantee success in meeting the challenges of the twenty-first century; abandoning them will certainly guarantee failure. But in order to increase the chances of success in applying policies of enlightened, principled self-interest, the UK needs more knowledge of the political contexts in which it operates and more modesty about its influence and what it can achieve. To paraphrase Kipling, Africa is not going to be developed after the methods of the West. There is too much Africa and she is too old.

Notes

1 The players

1 John Kampfner, *Blair's Wars* (London: Free Press, 2004), p. 64.

2 Robin Cook, interview with author, November 2004.

3 Intelligence reports that Saddam Hussein sought to obtain uranium from Niger were used to bolster the US/UK case for war in Iraq in early 2003. They were, however, subsequently discredited.

4 Ian Taylor, '"Advice is judged by results not by intentions": why Gordon Brown is wrong about Africa', *International Affairs*, 81(2) (2005), pp. 299–310.

5 DfID, *Eliminating Poverty: A Challenge for the 21st Century*, International Development White Paper (London: DfID, November 1997).

6 John Vereker, 'Blazing the trail: eight years of change in handling international development', *Development Policy Review*, 20(2) (2002), pp. 133–40.

7 Clare Short, *An Honourable Deception? New Labour, Iraq and the Misuse of Power* (London: Free Press, 2004), pp. 85–8.

8 Ibid., p. 78.

9 Robin Cook, interview with author, November 2004.

10 The expression 'new wars' was popularized by Mary Kaldor in her book *New and Old Wars:* *Organized Violence in a Global Era* (Cambridge: Polity Press, 1999). Kaldor was influential with Robin Cook.

11 Kampfner, *Blair's Wars*, p. 15.

12 Antony Goldman, 'Nigeria: many problems, few solutions', in Richard Haas (ed.), *Transatlantic Tensions* (Washington, DC: Brookings, 1999), p. 217.

13 Sir Thomas Legg and Sir Robin Ibbs, *Report of the Sierra Leone Arms Investigation* (London: Stationery Office, July 1998).

14 Short, *An Honourable Deception?*, p. 77.

15 Robin Cook, FCO mission statement, May 1997.

16 Tony Blair, speech delivered to the Lord Mayor's Banquet, November 1997.

17 Robert Cooper, *The Breaking of Nations: Order and Chaos in the Twenty-first Century* (London: Atlantic Books, 2003).

18 Tony Blair, quoted in Kampfner, *Blair's Wars*, p. 68.

19 Tony Blair, speech delivered to Chicago Economics Club, 22 April 1999.

20 Kampfner, *Blair's Wars*, p. 53.

21 The International Commission on Intervention and State

Sovereignty was to publish its findings in its 2001 report: *The Responsibility to Protect*.

22 The economist Irwin Steltzer referred to the speech admiringly as a classic neoconservative text: BBC Radio 4, *Start the Week*, 18 October 2004.

23 *Hansard* (Commons), 7 March 2001, col. 294.

24 Kampfner, *Blair's Wars*, p. 73.

25 David Margolick, profile of Tony Blair, *Vanity Fair*, May 2003.

26 Anthony Seldon, *Blair* (London: Free Press, 2005).

27 Tony Blair, speech in South Africa, 31 May 2007.

28 *The Economist* cover title, 12 May 2000.

29 Tony Blair, speech delivered to Labour Party conference, September 2001.

30 *Hansard*, 12 May 1999.

31 General Sir Rupert Smith, *The Utility of Force: The Art of War in the Modern World* (London: Allen Lane, 2005).

2 The policy

1 Tony Blair, statement at conclusion of Gleneagles G8 summit, 8 July 2005.

2 *Our Common Interest: Report of the Commission for Africa* (March 2005), p. 1.

3 Ibid., pp. 21–66.

4 Ibid., p. 65.

5 Ibid., p. 1.

6 Ibid., p. 106.

7 Ibid.

8 DfID White Paper, *Making Governance Work for the Poor*, July 2006.

9 *Our Common Interest*, p. 157.

10 Ibid., p. 182.

11 Ibid., p. 180.

12 Ibid., pp. 219ff.

13 Ibid., pp. 298–9.

14 Ibid., pp. 301ff.

15 Ibid., p. 328.

16 'The G8: what they said and what they meant', *Independent*, 9 June 2007.

17 *Our Common Interest*, p. 328.

18 Ibid., pp. 121–32.

19 Ibid., p. 125.

20 Ibid., p. 126.

21 Ibid., p. 127.

22 Carolyn Nordstrom, *Shadows of War: Violence, Power and International Profiteering in the Twenty-first Century* (Berkeley: University of California Press, 2004).

23 *Our Common Interest*, p. 132.

24 FCO White Paper, *Active Diplomacy for a Changing World: The UK's International Priorities*, March 2006. Priority 6 on climate change was added in June 2006.

25 *Our Common Interest*, p. 23.

26 *Active Diplomacy for a Changing World*, p. 34.

27 Ibid., p. 35.

28 Home Office Statistical Bulletin, *Asylum Statistics United Kingdom 2005*, 22 August 2006.

29 *Active Diplomacy for a Changing World*, pp. 15–16.

30 *Hansard*, 19 July 2004.

31 Derek Chollet, *Policy Review*, 114, August/September 2002.

32 Mark Malloch-Brown, speech at the Royal Geographical Society, London, June 2007.

3 Limits of leverage

1 The allocations cited in this section, including those in Table 3.1, are all drawn from DfID's annual departmental reports, 2001 and 2007.

2 William Easterly, 'The ideology of development', in *Foreign Policy*, July/August 2007.

3 DfID, *Partnerships for Poverty Reduction: Rethinking Conditionality* (London: DfID, 2005).

4 Peter Stothard, *30 Days: A Month at the Heart of Blair's War* (London: HarperCollins, 2003), p. 42.

5 See, for example, Tony Blair's address to Sierra Leonean troops, Freetown, 30 May 2007.

6 *Sierra Leone: The Election Opportunity*, International Crisis Group report, July 2007, p. i.

7 It is quite hard to work out how much of DfID's programme budget is spent supporting civil society.

8 Clare Short, interview with author, November 2004.

9 Ibid.

10 Clare Short, *An Honourable Deception? New Labour, Iraq and the Misuse of Power* (London: Free Press, 2004).

11 DfID, *Government, Development and Democratic Politics: DfID's Work in Building More Effective States* (London: DfID, 2007), p. 68.

4 Futures

1 Tony Blair, speech delivered to the Labour Party conference, September 2001.

2 Larry Elliot, 'We still haven't found what we're looking for', *Guardian*, 11 June 2007.

3 DfID, *Government, Development and Democratic Politics: DfID's Work in Building More Effective States* (London: DfID, 2007).

Further reading

Abrahamsen, Rita (2005) 'Blair's Africa: the politics of securitization and fear', *Alternatives: Global, Local, Political*, 30(1).

Abrahamsen, Rita and Paul Williams (2001) 'The antinomies of New Labour's third way in sub-Saharan Africa', *Political Studies*, 49.

Abse, Leo (2003) *Tony Blair: The Man Who Lost His Smile*, London: Robson.

Aldred, John (2002) *British Imperial and Foreign Policy, 1846–1980*, London: John Murray.

Beckett, Francis and David Hencke (2005) *The Survivor: Tony Blair in Peace and War*, London: Aurum Press.

Benthall, Jonathan (1993) *Disasters, Relief and the Media*, London: I.B.Tauris.

Boyce, D. George (1999) *Decolonization and the British Empire, 1775–1997*, London: Macmillan.

Calderisi, Robert (2006) *The Trouble with Africa: Why Foreign Aid isn't Working*, New York: Palgrave Macmillan.

Clarke, Michael (1992) *British External Policy-making in the 1990s*, London: Macmillan.

Commission for Africa (2005) *Our Common Interest: Report of the Commission for Africa*.

Cooper, Robert (2003) *The Breaking of Nations: Order and Chaos in the Twenty-first Century*, London: Atlantic Books.

Cradock, Percy (1997) *In Pursuit of British Interests: Reflections on Foreign Policy under Margaret Thatcher and John Major*, London: John Murray.

Darwin, John (1988) *Britain and Decolonisation: Retreat from Empire in the Post-war World*, London: Macmillan.

DfID (1997) *Eliminating Poverty: A Challenge for the 21st Century*, White Paper, London: DfID, November.

— (2005) *Why We Need to Work More Effectively in Fragile States*, Policy paper.

— (2006) *Making Governance Work for the Poor*, White Paper, London: DfID, July.

— (2007) *Government, Development and Democratic Politics: DfID's Work in Building More Effective States*, London: DfID.

Dickie, John (1992) *Inside the Foreign Office*, London: Chapmans.

— (2004) *The New Mandarins: How British Foreign Policy Works*, London: I.B. Tauris.

Duffield, Mark (2001) *Global Governance and the New Wars: The Merger of Development and Security*, London: Zed Books.

Easterly, William (2006) *The White Man's Burden: Why the West's Efforts to Aid the Rest Have Done so Much Ill and so Little Good*, New York: Penguin.

— (2007) 'The ideology of development', *Foreign Policy*, July/August.

FCO (2006) *Active Diplomacy for a Changing World: The UK's International Priorities*, FCO, White Paper, March.

Goldman, Antony (1999) 'Nigeria: many problems, few solutions', in Richard Haas (ed.), *Transatlantic Tensions*, Washington, DC: Brookings Institute.

Hemming, Philip E. (1996) 'Macmillan and the end of the British Empire in Africa', in Richard Aldous and Sabine Lee (eds), *Harold Macmillan and Britain's World Role*, London: Macmillan.

Hyam, Ronald (2006) *Britain's Declining Empire: The Road to Decolonisation 1918–1968*, Cambridge: CUP.

ICISS (2001) *The Responsibility to Protect: Report of the International Commission on Intervention and State Sovereignty.*

Kaldor, Mary (1999) *New and Old Wars: Organized Violence in a Global Era*, Cambridge: Polity Press.

Kampfner, John (2004) *Blair's Wars*, London: Free Press.

Legg, Sir Thomas and Sir Robin Ibbs (1998) *Report of the Sierra Leone Arms Investigation*, London: Stationery Office.

Louis, William Roger and Judith Brown (eds) (1999) *The Oxford History of the British Empire, Vol. IV: The Twentieth Century*, Oxford: OUP.

Nordstrom, Carolyn (2004) *Shadows of War: Violence, Power and International Profiteering in the Twenty-first Century*, Berkeley: University of California Press.

Porteous, Tom (2005) 'British government policy in sub-Saharan Africa under New Labour', *International Affairs*, 81(2).

Power, Samantha (2002) *A Problem from Hell: America and the Age of Genocide*, New York: Basic Books.

Rawnsley, Andrew (2000) *Servants of the People: The Inside Story of New Labour*, London: Hamish Hamilton.

Ross, Carne (2007) *Independent Diplomat: Dispatches from an Unaccountable Elite*, London: C. Hurst & Co.

Seldon, Anthony (2001) *The Blair Effect*, London: Little, Brown.

— (2005) *Blair*, London: Free Press.

Short, Clare (2004) *An Honourable Deception? New Labour, Iraq and the Misuse of Power*, London: Free Press.

Smith, General Sir Rupert (2005) *The Utility of Force: The Art of War in the Modern World*, London: Allen Lane.

Stothard, Peter (2003) *30 Days: A Month at the Heart of Blair's War*, London: HarperCollins.

Taylor, Ian (2005) '"Advice is judged by results not by intentions": why Gordon Brown is wrong about Africa', *International Affairs*, 81(2).

Vereker, John (2002) 'Blazing the trail: eight years of change in handling international development', *Development Policy Review*, 20(2): 133–40.

Williams, Paul (2004) 'Britain and Africa after the cold war: beyond damage limitation?', in Ian Taylor and Paul Williams (eds), *Africa in International Politics: External Involvement on the Continent*, London: Routledge.

— (2006) *British Foreign Policy under New Labour, 1997–2005*, London: Palgrave Macmillan.

Woods, Ngaire (2005) 'The shifting politics of foreign aid', *International Affairs*, 81(2).

Index